# INVITATION
## TO
# ROMANS

A Short-Term **DISCIPLE** Bible Study

# INVITATION TO ROMANS

## Pamela M. Eisenbaum

*Abingdon Press*
*Nashville*

A Short-Term DISCIPLE Bible Study

INVITATION TO ROMANS
*Copyright © 2006 by Abingdon Press*

Harriett Jane Olson, Senior Vice President of Publishing, and Editor of Church
School Publications; Mark Price, Senior Editor; Mickey Frith, Associate Editor;
Leo Ferguson, Designer; Kent Sneed, Design Manager

14 15 — 11
MANUFACTURED IN THE UNITED STATES OF AMERICA

# Contents

# Meet the Writers

**PAMELA M. EISENBAUM,** the writer of the commentary in each session, is Associate Professor of Biblical Studies and Christian Origins at the Iliff School of Theology in Denver, Colorado. She is also an associate faculty member of the Center for Judaic Studies at the University of Denver. She is the author of *The Jewish Heroes of Christian History: Hebrews 11 in Literary Context*, is a contributor to the *Women's Bible Commentary*, and has published several essays on ancient Judaism and Christianity. She appeared in the recent ABC documentary "Jesus and Paul: The Word and the Witness" and is currently writing a book on Paul.

Dr. Eisenbaum is a member of B'nai Havurah Synagogue in Denver, Colorado. In her spare time, she enjoys skiing, mountain biking, cooking, listening to her iPod, and visiting art museums.


**PHILLIP NALL,** the writer of the "Invitation to Discipleship" and "For Reflection" sections of each session, is a long-time Christian educator and curriculum writer living in Atlanta, Georgia. He has led DISCIPLE Bible studies in local congregations and has served as part of the national DISCIPLE leadership training team for nearly ten years. He is also the writer of the leader guide for this study.

# An Invitation to This Study

The study you are about to begin is one in a series of short-term, in-depth, small-group Bible studies based on the design of DISCIPLE Bible study. Like the series of long-term DISCIPLE studies, this study has been developed with these underlying assumptions:

• The Bible is the primary text of study.

• Preparation on the part of participants is expected.

• The study leader acts as a facilitator rather than as a lecturer.

• A weekly group session features small-group discussion.

• Video presentations by scholars set the Scriptures in context.

• Encouraging and enhancing Christian discipleship are the goals of study.

This participant book is your guide to the study and preparation you will do prior to the weekly group meeting. To establish a disciplined pattern of study, first choose a time and a place where you can read, take notes, reflect, and pray. Then choose a good study Bible.

## CHOOSING AND USING A STUDY BIBLE

Again, keep in mind that the Bible is *the* text for all short-term DISCIPLE Bible studies, not the participant book; the function of the participant book is to help persons read and listen to the Bible. So because the Bible is the key to this study, consider a couple of recommendations in choosing a good study version of the Bible.

## First: The Translation

The recommended translation is the New Revised Standard Version (NRSV). It is recommended for two reasons: (1) It is a reliable, accurate translation, and (2) it is used in the preparation of all DISCIPLE study manuals.

However, any reliable translation can be used. In fact, having available several different translations is a good practice. Some of them include the NIV, NJB, REB, RSV, NKJV, and NAB. To compare the many English translations of the Bible before choosing, consider consulting the book *The Bible in English Translation: An Essential Guide*, by Steven M. Sheeley and Robert N. Nash, Jr. (Abingdon Press, 1997).

Keep in mind that the *Living Bible* and *The Message*, while popular versions of the Bible, are not considered translations. They are paraphrases.

For this study of Romans in particular, a study Bible that includes the Apocrypha will be useful. The Apocrypha is a term used to describe the collection of Old Testament books considered canonical by Catholic and Orthodox churches but noncanonical by Protestants and Jews.

## Second: The Study Features

The recommended Bible to use in any study is, of course, a study Bible— that is, a Bible containing notes, introductions to each book, charts, maps, and other helps designed to deepen and enrich the study of the biblical text. Because there are so many study Bibles available today, be sure to choose one based on some basic criteria:

- The introductory articles to each book or group of books are helpful to you in summarizing the main features of those books.

- The notes illuminate the text of Scripture by defining words, making cross-references to similar passages, and providing cultural or historical background. Keep in mind that the mere volume of notes is not necessarily an indication of their value.

- The maps, charts, and other illustrations display important biblical/historical data in a way that is accurate and accessible.

- Any glossaries, dictionaries, concordances, or indexes in the Bible are easily located and understood.

To a greater or lesser degree, all study Bibles attempt to strike a balance between *interpreting* for the reader what the text means and *helping* the reader understand what the text says. Study Bible notes are conveyed through the interpretive lens of those who prepare the notes. However, regardless of what study Bible you choose to use, always be mindful of which part of the page is Scripture and which part is not.

# GETTING THE MOST FROM READING THE BIBLE

Read the Bible with curiosity. Ask the questions *Who? What? Where? When? How?* and *Why?* as you read.

Learn as much as you can about the passage you are studying. Try to discover what the writer was saying for the time in which the passage was written. Be familiar with the surrounding verses and chapters to establish a passage's setting or situation.

Pay attention to the form of a passage of Scripture. How you read and understand poetry or a parable will differ from how you read and understand a historical narrative.

Above all, let the Scripture speak for itself, even if the apparent meaning is troubling or unclear. Question the Scripture, but also seek answers to your questions in the Scripture itself. Often the biblical text will solve some of the problems that arise in certain passages. Consult additional reference resources when needed. And remember to trust the Holy Spirit to guide you in your study.

# MAKING USE OF ADDITIONAL RESOURCES

Though you will need only the Bible and this participant book to have a meaningful experience, these basic reference books may help you go deeper into your study of Scripture:

- *Eerdmans Dictionary of the Bible*, edited by David Noel Freedman (William B. Eerdmans Publishing Company, 2000).

- *Eerdmans Commentary on the Bible*, edited by James D. G. Dunn and John W. Rogerson (William B. Eerdmans Publishing Company, 2003).

- *Romans in Full Circle: A History of Interpretation*, by Mark Reasoner (Westminster John Knox Press, 2005).

- *Final Account: Paul's Letter to the Romans*, by Krister Stendahl (Augsburg Fortress, 1995).

- *The Theology of Paul the Apostle*, by James D. G. Dunn (Wm. B. Eerdmans Publishing Co., 1998).

- *Dictionary of Paul and His Letters*, edited by Gerald F. Hawthorne, Ralph P. Martin, and Daniel G. Reid (InterVarsity Press, 1993).

- *The New Interpreter's Bible: A Commentary in Twelve Volumes*, Vol. X, the commentary on Romans (Abingdon Press, 2002).

- *Ancient Christian Commentary on Scripture, New Testament VI: Romans*, edited by Gerald Bray (InterVarsity Press, 1998).

# MAKING USE OF THE PARTICIPANT BOOK

The participant book serves two purposes. First, it is your study guide: Use it to structure your daily reading of the assigned Scripture passages and to prompt your reflection on what you read. Second, it is your note-taking journal: Use it to write down any insights, comments, and questions you want to recall and perhaps make use of in your group's discussions.

The commentary is full of references to the assigned readings from the Bible and was prepared by a writer who assumed his or her readers would be knowledgeable of the week's Scriptures before coming to the commentary. So the recommended approach to this study is to let the biblical writers have their say first. In fact, in this study of Romans, you will be directed to let Paul have his say twice: On Day 6, the assignment is to read the week's Romans passages a second time through.

Throughout the commentary, you will notice certain words or phrases in **boldface type.** These should direct you to corresponding text, which appears in a gray-toned Roman coin image nearby, with information defining or elaborating upon those words or phrases. In other instances, the Roman coin image contains stand-out text pulled from the commentary.

Following the commentary is an "Invitation to Discipleship" page designed to facilitate reflection on the week's readings as well as "For Reflection" questions and space for your responses. Time to discuss these questions and your responses is built into the weekly group meeting.

# Introduction

It is difficult to overstate the importance of Romans in Christian tradition. Were it not for Romans, the early church father **Augustine,** the Bishop of Hippo, would never have become a Christian; and without Romans 5 in particular, he might never have conceived the doctrine of original sin. Were it not for Romans 13, the great Protestant Reformer **Martin Luther** could not have formulated a vision in which church authority and political governance were given respectful independence. Were it not for Romans 9, **John Calvin,** the shaper of Reformed theology, could never have worked out so elaborate a doctrine of predestination. Were it not for Luther's commentary *Preface to the Epistle to the Romans,* **John Wesley,** Methodism's founder, might never have left Aldersgate-Street with a "heart strangely warmed" and a vision for church renewal. Were it not for Romans as a whole, a host of Protestant Reformers might never have contributed to the doctrine of justification by faith, the cornerstone of Protestant Christianity to this day. Were it not for Romans, Christians would not know these moving, memorable words that have given comfort and hope to countless people who would otherwise suffer in despair: "For...neither death, nor life, nor angels, nor rulers, nor things present, nor things to come, nor powers, nor height, nor depth, nor anything else in all creation, will be able to separate us from the love of God in Christ Jesus our Lord" (Romans 8:38-39). In other words, had Romans not been preserved as part of the New Testament canon, Christianity might look very different than it does today.

Therefore, serious study of Paul's Letter to the Romans does more than simply give us insight into the biblical text and the theology of Paul. Such study is a lens through which we can reflect on the history of Christianity. Indeed, reading Romans can teach us about some of the key components of Christian identity—components that many Christians take for granted, do not fully understand, or fail to notice. At the same time, precisely because Romans has been so influential in the development of Christian doctrine, it is difficult for Christians to read it with clear eyes. Paul's teachings in Romans come to us mediated through the greatest theologians of the church. Many of us are likely to *read* Paul but *hear* Luther. Because so many essential Christian doctrines are grounded in Paul's Letter to the Romans, we tend to assume that Paul himself is the author of these doctrines. As a result, it is difficult for us to engage in our own interpretive conversation with the text. But in reality, these doctrines were worked out by thoughtful Christians of ages past (like Luther) who studied Paul's words and then interpreted those words in ways so compelling that they not only reinvigorated their own faith, they also inspired seismic reforms in the church.

Augustine, Luther, and Calvin (among others) were active—perhaps even *activist*—interpreters of Scripture. These great fathers of the church are excellent models for modern Christian readers who want to engage in serious Bible study. They viewed Scripture as the living Word of God, accepting that God's Word was authoritative. For them, this meant finding a way to embody the Word of God individually and communally. In the case of Paul's letters, especially Romans, they viewed the apostle's teachings as subtle, sophisticated, and complex—meaning they recognized (as we often do) that sometimes Paul was hard to understand! And in most cases, the church's theologians carried on a lifelong conversation with Paul, and whatever insights came from such conversations, they brought them to bear on the important theological issues of the day.

The challenge we face as students of Romans today is learning to engage in our own interpretive conversation with the text, in spite of the deeply entrenched tradition of interpretation that provides ready-made answers to a set of predetermined questions. For example, consider this: Augustine's understanding of Romans became dominant because his reflections on his own experience of religious transformation (which he grounded in Romans) initiated the modern Western notion of the self. In particular, Augustine's reflections on his inner spiritual life became a model for understanding the interior drama played out by every new convert to Christianity. That is, he simultaneously redefined what it meant to be human and what it meant to be Christian.

But Augustine's definition marked a gigantic shift from the way ancient Jews, Greeks, Romans, and others thought about human nature in general and the religious dimension of being human in particular. Prior to Augustine, Christian commentaries on Romans were considerably more varied than they would become later. We find in **Origen,** a third-century theologian, an alternative tradition of interpretation markedly different from Augustine. Unfortunately, this alternative tradition was practically lost to oblivion because of what came to be the overwhelming dominance of the Augustinian tradition. One of the aims of this study of Romans is to introduce a way of reading Romans that challenges the Augustinian point of view. Significantly, this way of reading Romans finds resonance in the strain of interpretation associated not just with Origen of the third century but also with recent Pauline scholarship of the last thirty years. As we go along, be on the lookout for several points of emphasis that distinguish this alternative perspective on Romans from the traditional one.

- Romans is oriented toward communal rather than individual salvation.

- The central message of Romans is God-centered, not Christ-centered.

- Romans is written by a Jew who believes in Jesus, but a Jew nevertheless.

- Romans addresses a Gentile audience.

- Romans is primarily concerned with the relationship between Jews and Gentiles and the relationship of both to God.

- Romans is a guide for living a faithful life in an age of religious pluralism.

It may also be helpful to keep in mind that recent challenges to the prevailing Augustinian perspective on Romans have in part been inspired by post-Holocaust reflection as well as improved knowledge of ancient Judaism. Early on in the church's history, the traditional reading of Romans both depended on and contributed to a distorted picture of Judaism. Another aim of this study is to promote a more historically accurate understanding of ancient Judaism and thereby a reconsideration of the meaning of Romans for today. Hopefully, studying Romans in this spirit will break down old stereotypes of Judaism and inspire fresh reflection on Christianity.

**Origen (c. 185–c. 254)**
Christian theologian from Alexandria who
wrote the earliest extant commentary on Romans

**Augustine (354–430)**
Bishop of Hippo whose writings on sin, grace, and
predestination profoundly shaped church doctrine in the West

**Martin Luther (1483–1546)**
monk, priest, theologian who founded the German Reformation
and completed a German translation of the Bible

**John Calvin (1509–1564)**
founder of the Protestant Reformation in Geneva whose
writings formed the basis for Reformed theology

**John Wesley (1703–1791)**
Anglican clergyman, missionary, theologian
who founded the Methodist movement

# An Orientation to Romans

*For I will not venture to speak of anything except
what Christ has accomplished through me to win obedience
from the Gentiles, by word and deed.*

—Romans 15:18

## INTRODUCTION

Context is essential in the interpretation of any document, and this is no less true for biblical texts. So to begin this study, let's situate Romans in two ways: in its scriptural context and in its historical setting. This week's readings from the Old Testament demonstrate the way in which God speaks to those who are willing to listen through specially chosen figures. Prophetic figures like Moses do not merely communicate knowledge of the divine will; their stories provide instructions about how people should respond to God both individually and communally. They also provide warnings about the consequences of disobeying God. Some key themes about the divine-human relationship that appear in the Old Testament texts recur in Romans.

The first and last chapters of Romans provide substantial information not only about the circumstances prompting Paul to write this letter but also about Paul's understanding of his mission more broadly. Whatever image of Paul subsequent readers may hold in their mind's eye, Paul first and foremost thinks of himself as the apostle to the Gentiles. As he tells us in Galatians 1:11-17, the revelation of Jesus that Paul experienced was God's way of communicating to Paul his apostolic mission.

# DAILY ASSIGNMENTS

The first week's readings set Romans in context in two ways: (1) The readings from Paul's letters provide historical information about Paul's personal experiences, his mission, and his reasons for writing Romans. (2) The readings from the Old Testament give a sense of the Scriptures that influenced Paul's life and thought.

## DAY ONE: Deuteronomy 4:1-40; Isaiah 40:1–41:10

Compare the characterization of God in these two divine speeches from the Old Testament. Note the way in which God is portrayed as the Lord of the universe, the only true God, who nevertheless privileges Israel above the other nations.

## DAY TWO: Romans 1; 15:14–16:27

What kinds of historical information do these framing chapters of Romans provide about Paul's personal experience, about his missionary accomplishments thus far, and about his plans for the future?

**DAY THREE: Wisdom of Solomon 13–14**

One of the books of the Apocrypha, the Wisdom of Solomon is a Hellenistic Jewish text likely written at the same time Paul was writing his letters. It provides a classic example of the Jewish polemic against idolatry.

**DAY FOUR: Jeremiah 1:4-10; Isaiah 49:1-6; Galatians 1:11-17**

In what ways does Paul's Damascus road experience resemble (or not) the call of Israel's most celebrated prophets?

**DAY FIVE: Commentary**

Read the commentary in the participant book.

**DAY SIX: Romans 1; 15:14–16:27**

Reread the week's selection from Romans in light of the other assigned texts and the commentary.

# APOSTLE TO THE GENTILES

The salutation that opens Paul's Letter to the Romans is much longer than those found in the other **undisputed Pauline Epistles.** Usually Paul names himself as the sender of the letter, with only a brief description of himself as an "apostle" or "servant"; he then promptly names the addressees, to whom he offers greetings of "grace" and "peace." The opening of Romans is more than a salutation; it functions as a kind a summary statement of the letter. As such, it captures in condensed form Paul's two-fold purpose: to explain his reasons for undertaking a mission to the Gentiles and to share his vision for the future messianic age.

**Thirteen letters in the New Testament are attributed to Paul. Only seven of them are considered "undisputed"—Romans, First & Second Corinthians, Galatians, Philippians, First Thessalonians, and Philemon—meaning most biblical scholars today affirm them to be authentically from Paul's hand.**

Paul says in Romans 1:1-2 that he is "called to be an apostle, set apart for the gospel of God," and invokes the "prophets in the holy scriptures" who proclaimed God's promises in ages past. This connection between Paul's apostleship and Israel's prophets provides the first key to understanding Paul's sense of his mission as an apostle. After several descriptive phrases about God's Son, Paul circles back to apostleship (1:5), and here he explicitly reveals the purpose of his mission—namely, "to bring about the obedience of faith among all the Gentiles." This phrase is the second key to understanding Paul's identity as an apostle and to understanding the overall thrust of Romans. Importantly, the same language occurs in the concluding chapters. Paul speaks of winning "obedience from the Gentiles" (15:18), and embedded in the culminating doxology that closes the letter, the identical phrase "the obedience of faith" appears again (16:26). This last instance is striking, for at the same time Paul praises God, the apostle invokes his own role in the divine plan. The doxology also mentions "the prophetic writings" through which "the mystery that was kept secret for long ages" is now being revealed "to all the Gentiles." Thus, like the opening address, the concluding doxology reads like a recap of Romans, creating a kind of frame that draws our attention to the main theme of Romans: Paul's theology of mission.

To unpack this theme, we first need a fuller grasp of Paul's understanding of himself as an apostle. The Greek word *apostolos* can be defined simply as "one who is sent out" to accomplish a mission. But in the context of the early church, Paul is not like the other apostles. He is not one of the twelve appointed by Jesus according to gospel tradition and cannot be counted among any of Jesus' disciples. What really sets Paul apart from the other apostles is that he never knew Jesus in human form. His first experience of Jesus is as the risen Christ made known to him through divine revelation. This experience results in Paul's religious transformation. He becomes a believer in the Lord Jesus Christ. For this reason, Paul is known as the first convert to Christianity. His experience of Jesus becomes a model for the subsequent generations of Christians who would never know the human Jesus either and whose faith is based exclusively on the experience of the risen Christ. While it is absolutely clear that Paul had some kind of mystical, transformative experience of the risen Lord, the image of Paul as a convert can be an obstacle to comprehending his identity as apostle to the Gentiles, not to mention his continuing identity as a Jew. Usually, when we talk about conversion, we mean a change from one religion to another or from no religion to some kind of religion. Since Paul continues to refer to himself as a Jew after his encounter with Christ, it is misleading to call his experience a conversion. The image of Paul as the first convert to Christianity comes largely from the Book of Acts, which recounts the story no less than three times and includes many miraculous details. Unfortunately, Paul explicitly tells of this life-changing event only once (Galatians 1:11-17).

Paul's account is brief, but if we privilege Paul's version over Acts (written a half century or more later), then the experience looks more like God's call of a prophet than a religious conversion (**Galatians 1:15-17**). Not only does the language of being "set apart" and "called" resonate with Romans 1:1, but it also echoes the prophetic

> "But when God, who had set me apart before I was born and called me through his grace, was pleased to reveal his Son to me, so that I might proclaim him among the Gentiles, I did not confer with any human being, nor did I go up to Jerusalem to those who were already apostles before me, but I went away at once into Arabia, and afterwards I returned to Damascus."
> (*Galatians 1:15-17*)

call language found in Jeremiah (1:5) and Isaiah (49:1-6). This means that Paul's personal religious transformation from being a non-believer to a believer in Christ is linked to the very moment God appoints him apostle to the nations. The only way the language of conversion properly describes Paul's experience is that at some point in his life, he goes from being a persecutor of Jesus' followers to being a follower of Jesus. But that is exactly the same point at which he becomes God's apostle, specially chosen to preach the gospel to Gentiles. Thus, it seems more accurate to speak of Paul's experience of the risen Christ as a transformation, not a conversion. The language of transformation has the advantage of allowing us to see just what kind of change Paul experienced; for this change had less to do with his personal religious convictions than with his altered perception of what God wanted him to do—namely, transform the world by delivering a prophetic message to the Gentiles.

# PAUL'S AUDIENCE

Remember that Paul expresses his mission to the Gentiles in Romans 1:5 when he says he has "received grace and apostleship to bring about the obedience of faith among all the Gentiles." Then in 1:7, 13-15, Paul makes explicit that he regards those to whom he is writing in Rome as Gentiles. So it makes sense that he first turns his attention, in the body of Romans, to the condition of the Gentiles: They are idolaters who have not known God. Altogether, it seems reasonable to say that the audience in Paul's Letter to the Romans is Gentile. However, much of what Paul says later in Romans (especially Chapters 2–4 and 9–11) has traditionally been understood as a kind of "dialogue with Judaism" in which the apostle provides the rationale not merely for his mission but also for the validity of Christianity over against Judaism. So if Romans *is* a dialogue with Judaism, should we not assume the audience is Jewish rather than Gentile? In Romans 2:17, for example, Paul appears to address Jews explicitly: "But if you call yourself a Jew and rely on the law...." In sum, there appears to be an internal contradiction in Romans concerning the makeup of the audience. Sometimes Paul signals he is talking to Jews and sometimes to Gentiles.

In attempting to sort out the audience question, scholars often rely on the information in Romans 15, along with evidence from other sources, to get a picture of what prompted Paul to write Romans. It is clear from the letter itself that Paul is not the one who first brought the gospel to Rome, so the question of how the message about Christ got to Rome remains a mystery. All of Paul's other letters are written to communities that he founded, and they are occasioned by circumstances, questions, and concerns that arise after Paul's initial contact with them. Not so with Romans. The question remains, then: Why did Paul write to a community he did not found and did not visit?

Some scholars believe Paul's reference to the Jerusalem collection in Romans 15:25-33 is key. There, Paul seems apprehensive about even mentioning taking the collection to the saints in Jerusalem. With that in mind, and assuming there is a close connection between the type of Christianity in Rome and that in Jerusalem, it is conceivable that Paul writes to the Romans as a form of insurance for his journey to Jerusalem. He wants their support in the hope that they will insure his success when he delivers the offering to the saints in Jerusalem.

But then there is Paul's mention of his plans to go to Spain after Jerusalem in 15:28. Going into territory in the far western Mediterranean, as yet uncharted by any Christian missionaries, Paul will need a supply base. Perhaps he writes this letter hoping that when he comes to Rome on his way to Spain, the Roman church will provide the necessary support to make this ambitious mission to the West possible.

Of course, these two scenarios are not mutually exclusive. Paul may well have been writing both to alert the Roman community of his travels to Jerusalem *and* to prepare them for his subsequent visit on his way west. Yet in either case, a question emerges: If Paul's real motivation for writing Romans is to garner support for his work, why does he wait fifteen chapters to say what he wants? Besides, Chapter 15 is not terribly helpful in answering the question about who his audience is anyway.

However, a third perspective would simply take Paul at face value: Since he explicitly identifies as Gentiles the addressees to whom he writes in Romans, we may confidently assume that the audience Paul targets his letter to is, indeed, Gentile. Of course, the vast majority of readers of Romans over the subsequent centuries since its composition have *not* been people whom Paul could have envisioned when he wrote Romans. This only adds to the communication gap between biblical author and modern reader. Therefore, a word is in order about what exactly Paul means by the term *Gentiles*.

# WHO ARE THE GENTILES?

The word *Gentile* is used to translate the Greek word *ethnos*; *ethne* is the plural form. In ancient Jewish literature, the word can be translated either as "Gentiles" or "nations." Occasionally in Romans, translators render the word *ethne* as "nations" rather than "Gentiles," but most often it is rendered as "Gentiles" (Romans 2:14). For the majority of Greek-speaking people in antiquity, including Greek-speaking Jews, *ethnos* meant "nation" or "people." But ancient Jewish writers also used the word in a special sense, namely, as a designation for any and all people who were not Jewish. From the Jewish point of view, the world is essentially divided into two groups: Jews and Gentiles. Although modern readers usually operate within the categories of Jews and Christians when reading Paul, Paul himself never compares Jews and Christians. The word *Christian* had not yet been invented. However, like most any Jew of his day, Paul frequently contrasts Jews and Gentiles. To be sure, there are places where Paul contrasts believers with non-believers (15:30-31), and when he does, those terms cut across the categories of Jew and Gentile. That is to say, any given believer in Jesus may be either a Jew or Gentile. But those are the two most important categories for understanding Paul's message in Romans. The main difference between Jew and Gentile is that the latter does not know the one, true, living God. As Paul explains in Romans 1, the Gentiles became alienated from God through their idolatrous practices.

Thus, Paul's self-understanding as apostle to the Gentiles means that he customizes his message to meet the special needs and circumstances of the Gentiles. He himself did not become a Gentile; he writes as a Jew—a Jew speaking to Gentiles to be sure—but Paul maintains a Jewish perspective throughout his life.

# GENTILES AS IDOLATERS

One aspect of Romans that stands out most is its emphasis on the character of God. The repeated use of similarly structured phrases invoking God in the opening chapters of Romans emphasizes just how focused on God Paul is in his letter: "the gospel of God, "the power of God," "the righteousness of God," "the wrath of God," "the judgment of God," "the glory of God," among others. In fact, the word *God* appears well over a hundred times in Romans alone! Of course, Paul invokes the "Lord Jesus Christ" too, but there is no doubt the emphasis of this letter is on God, and Paul's rhetoric in these first few chapters is designed to direct our attention toward God.

At the very same time, the first chapter is an unequivocally harsh statement about how Gentiles have failed to recognize the God whom Paul is proclaiming. Paul's words amount to an indictment against the Gentiles—that is, against all nations except Israel—who from time immemorial have been guilty of the worst imaginable sin: idolatry. For a Hellenistic Jew like Paul, idolatry is defined as the worship of false gods or of anything or anyone who purports to represent a god. It is the sin of sins, the sin that leads to all other sins. (Compare Romans 1:18-32 to Wisdom of Solomon 13 and 14. Other tirades against idolatry appear in Jeremiah 10:1-16; Isaiah 44:9-20; and Psalm 135:15-18.)

The practice of idolatry is the critical feature that distinguishes Gentile from Jew. According to Hellenistic writers like Philo and **Josephus** (and contrary to modern assumptions), exclusive devotion to the one God of Israel is more important in determining Jewish identity than whether or not one is born a Jew. Even though other Jewish writers contemporary with Paul point out that the great philosophers of ancient Greece recognized the truth of monotheism, Jews were distinguished in Greco-Roman antiquity by their exclusive devotion to their one and only God. There can be no doubt that Paul's gospel included teaching Gentiles to adhere to this brand of monotheism; for it is from this theological base that Paul moves to address how and why the Lord Jesus Christ fits into his gospel.

> "To all who desire to come and live under the same laws with us,...it is not family ties alone which constitute relationship, but agreement in the principles of conduct."[1]
> *(Josephus)*

# INVITATION TO DISCIPLESHIP

In Isaiah 40, we read that God's glory will be revealed when every valley is lifted, every mountain made low, the uneven level, and the rough places plain. Impatient, we often set our own standards through which God is revealed to us and end up worshiping and serving something other than the Creator. Part of what Paul is saying in the early chapters of Romans is that human nature tends toward idolatry. Then Paul sets about to explain just what God—whose nature is righteous—has done about that. One of the invitations Paul issues through Romans is for us to recognize and understand this profound chasm between human nature and God's nature.

Also, in both the opening and the closing of Romans, Paul proclaims the purpose of his mission to the Gentiles: "to bring about the obedience of faith" (1:5; 16:26). At the same time, Paul claims authority as one set apart to carry out that mission. Implied in those two claims is another invitation: to participate with Paul in faith and in mission. By pointing to a God who has spoken and continues to speak through specially chosen figures, by pointing to a God who is both jealous and merciful, and by pointing to a God who has acted to bring salvation "to the Jew first and also to the Greek" (1:16), Paul invites us to hear and believe this "gospel of God" and to take that gospel to the nations.

# FOR REFLECTION

- In Romans, the word *God* appears well over a hundred times. In light of your study this week, how would you describe Paul's understanding of the nature of God? What is your understanding of the nature of God?

- Paul expresses his desire "to bring about the obedience of faith" among the Gentiles. What does this mean?

- How would you explain the difference between conversion and transformation? How would you describe the change that occurred in Paul's life as a result of his encounter with Christ? What can Paul's experience with Christ teach us about our own religious experiences?

# The Righteousness of God and the Faith of Jesus

*But now, apart from law, the righteousness of God has been disclosed, and is attested by the law and the prophets, the righteousness of God through faith in Jesus Christ for all who believe.*

—Romans 3:21-22

## INTRODUCTION

Regardless of how familiar we are with Romans, traditional assumptions will undoubtedly play a role in our reading of the letter's early chapters. Why? Because Romans 1–3 represents the very core of Pauline theology as reflected in the history of Western thought. Remember that Romans traditionally has been understood as a dialogue with Judaism. Yet, in the previous lesson, we were introduced to the idea that Paul's primary audience should actually be understood as Gentiles. Of course, it is possible that Paul is addressing a topic "in dialogue" with Judaism without necessarily implying that the audience to whom he imagines himself speaking is comprised of Jews. In any case, it is important not to assume too readily that the presence of a certain subject matter automatically points to a certain kind of audience.

So with that in mind, read Romans 2–3 while imagining that Paul is speaking to Gentiles. He may well be speaking to them about Judaism, Jewish law, the Jewish God, and Jewish Scripture. But even so, imagine that his words are directed to Gentiles. Then ask yourself a question: *When we consider to whom Paul is speaking, how does this affect the way we interpret his words?*

# DAILY ASSIGNMENTS

As you read this week's Scriptures, make note of any familiar phrases or verses you often hear repeated by Christian teachers, preachers, or lay people. For each one you note, ask yourself, *Do I have a good grasp of what it means?* Many of the most familiar verses are often the ones most vigorously debated by interpreters.

## DAY ONE: Deuteronomy 10:12-20; 32:1-9

In both these excerpts from Deuteronomy, the covenantal bond between God and Israel emphasizes the connection between divine and human righteousness.

## DAY TWO: Romans 2

Note especially the positive comments Paul makes about Jewish law.

## DAY THREE: Romans 3

Does Romans 3 seem to build on what was said in Romans 2, or does it seem to flow in another—perhaps even contradictory—direction?

## DAY FOUR: Psalms 14–15; 96

Note the way these psalms echo the two themes emphasized in the readings from Deuteronomy and Romans: that God is the only God and that God's righteousness is unimpeachable.

## DAY FIVE: Commentary

Read the commentary in the participant book.

## DAY SIX: Romans 2–3

Reflect on the week's selections from Romans in light of the Old Testament texts and the commentary, especially with regard to the theme of righteousness, both as it pertains to God and to humans.

# DIVINE JUDGMENT AND HUMAN ACCOUNTABILITY

The second and third chapters of Romans continue a theme already introduced in the first chapter—namely, the righteousness of God in relation to human accountability. Together, these opening chapters speak ominously of God's coming condemnation. Because traditional assumptions are unconsciously operating for most of us as we read what Paul has to say about God's condemnation, it is helpful to name these assumptions explicitly.

- All human beings are sinners, because sin is characteristic of human nature.

- Because every human being is a sinner, God is justified in executing a sentence of universal condemnation.

- Therefore, God renders the same guilty verdict on everyone alike, Jew and Gentile, slave and free, male and female.

On the one hand, Paul is assumed to be potentially addressing everyone, or at least every Christian. References to Jew and Gentile can be taken as Paul's shorthand for referring to all of humanity. And what Paul says is assumed to apply to everyone in the same way. After all, sin is a universal human problem that originated with Adam. But on the other hand, Paul's target audience is generally understood to be Jews, because Christian interpreters have imagined that Jews viewed themselves as both morally superior and specially favored by God. In that case, Paul's message of universal condemnation is really intended to communicate to Jews that they are as sinful as Gentiles, if not more so.

Of course, a traditional reading of Romans would emphasize that Paul's point in bringing his readers to a realization of God's universal condemnation is not to leave them in a state of hopeless despair but rather to present *the* universal solution to *the* universal problem. That solution is first articulated in Romans 1:16-17 when the "righteousness of God" is first mentioned. The fuller statement—about the righteousness of God as salvation "for all who believe"—is found in 3:21-26. There, the righteousness of God that Paul says is now being revealed and the "redemption that is in Christ Jesus" are one in the same.

Along with his emphasis on the righteousness of God, the traditional reading of Romans views Paul as also concerned about proclaiming the necessity of Christ as rooted in Genesis 3, where Adam's first sin turns all humans into disobedient sinners. Even though Paul does not mention Adam in the opening chapters of Romans, we assume the story of the Fall underlies his discussion. Of course, as modern readers, we live in a world in which the **doctrine of original sin** is assumed as a self-evident truth about human nature. (It is also frequently assumed, though mistakenly, that Paul is the first to articulate this doctrine.) Generally speaking, human nature is understood today to be inherently, inescapably sinful, and there is nothing any human being of any sort—Jew or Greek—can do to become righteous in God's sight. Paul's conclusion seems to follow: God must impute righteousness to them through an act of vicarious atonement. That is why Christ is necessary. Thus, this traditional reading of Romans 1–3 defines both the common Western notion of human nature and the common Christian understanding of salvation. This interpretation of Paul comes to us as part of our Christian heritage; and it is part of the reason why it is difficult for us to see Romans any other way.

Called in Latin *peccatum originale*, the doctrine of original sin developed out of the teachings of early-church fathers like Augustine (appealing especially to Romans 5:12-21), Aquinas, and later Reformers. The doctrine defines all humankind as inevitably sinful as a result of Adam's first disobedience.

However, there is another way to read Romans 1–3. It calls for us to give careful consideration to everything Paul is saying in these opening chapters. First, notice how he places threats of God's judgment next to reminders of God's mercy for those who are moved to repentance (2:4-5). Then look at Paul's statements in 2:6 and 2:13: It sounds as though there *are* distinctions within the great mass of humanity—that not everyone is equally deserving of God's condemnation, but rather God judges people according to their works and rewards them accordingly (2:6). Consider in particular 2:13: "For it is not the hearers of the law who are righteous in God's sight, but the doers of the law who will be justified." The *doers of the law* will be justified? Does that sound like Paul?

In fact, in Romans 2:1-16, Paul appears to argue the opposite of what virtually all commentators say he argues in the first three chapters of Romans. Recall that a traditional reading of Paul takes as his main point that everyone—Jew and Gentile alike—stands in such a state of sinful degradation that nothing they could possibly do can save them from the coming wrath of God, hence the need for Christ. But to the contrary, Romans 2:1-15 distinguishes between people who do good (2:7) and those who do evil (2:9). Furthermore, God rewards those who do good and punishes those who do evil (2:7-10). Perhaps divine impartiality does not mean that God renders the same condemnation on everyone, Jew and Gentile alike. Perhaps God judges everyone by the same standard, even the same *law*.

Perhaps. But even if Paul does not regard Jews and Gentiles as possessed of the same moral capacity in general, he believes individual Gentiles are capable of living according to God's law—not because they study the Torah but because they have God's law written on their hearts. Hellenistic Jews believed that the Torah was both the unique possession of Jews, a constitution regulating the lives of Jews, as well as the perfect manifestation of God's universal wisdom, an ethical code and source of divine instruction applicable to everyone. Thus, it is easily conceivable to Paul that some Gentiles possess an internal moral compass allowing them to lead righteous lives. They demonstrate that God's law is written on their hearts (2:14-15). Conversely, some Jews, in spite of having the advantage of Torah, do not lead moral lives (2:17-25). Again, we may draw two conclusions from these observations: First, everyone—whether Jew or Gentile—has the same basic human nature, and that nature is *not* hopelessly depraved. Everyone has the capacity to do good or to do evil. Second, Jews may have been entrusted with the Torah, but all people are morally accountable—that is, accountable to the law of God. Jews are not some kind of selective breed of humans, but they do have the advantage of being chosen as God's "treasured possession" (Deuteronomy 7:6). As a result, Israel possesses a covenant with God in which God has made promises of eternal allegiance, and in return Israel devotes herself to God's service. In sum, Jews have enjoyed the privilege of knowing God in a way that sets them apart from Gentile nations. In other words, the issue of accountability is much greater for Gentiles, collectively speaking, than for Jews.

# SALVATION AND FAITH

The last verses of Romans 3 are arguably the most important verses in the Christian Bible. They have also been commented on quite heavily over the last two thousand years. Most influential has been the commentary of Martin Luther, the great Protestant Reformer of the sixteenth century. Although **Luther's famed tower experience** is associated with Romans 1:16-17, he perceived Romans 3:21-28 to be an encapsulation of the master narrative of the Bible. So the Bible for Luther became the story of the Fall, of the incapacity of humans to do anything good, and of the incalculable debt of accumulated sin of generations past that could only be removed by Christ's sacrificial death. Luther understood the mention of divine forbearance in passing over previously committed sins (3:25) as referring not to the sins of idolatrous Gentiles who had not known God or to wicked individuals (Jew or Gentile) but *to every human being who ever lived*; for every human being except Christ is a sinner for whom no act of penance will suffice. The biblical story teaches that salvation can only come by a radical act of divine intervention. Human beings must recognize they have no part to play in their own salvation except to receive the righteousness imputed to them by God through Jesus Christ. In more familiar terms, people can only be saved by faith in Jesus. Faith in Christ is the only means by which a human being is justified, and justification—which is just another name for attaining a state of righteousness—is a prerequisite for being saved. As a result of this contribution from Martin Luther, Protestant Christianity's foundation was established.

> "At last, by the mercy of God, meditating day and night, I gave heed to the context of the words [of Romans 1:17], namely, 'In it the righteousness of God is revealed, as it is written, "He who through faith is righteous shall live."' There I began to understand that the righteousness of God is that by which the righteous lives by a gift of God, namely by faith.... Thus that place in Paul was for me truly the gate to paradise."[2]
> *(Martin Luther)*

Another of Luther's contributions to Protestantism came by way of his famous German translation of the New Testament, in which he added a small but enormously influential word to his rendering of Romans 3:28. That word was *allein*, "alone." Thanks to the insertion of the word *allein* in the German Bible, Romans became a treatise on justification by faith, in which "a person is justified by faith" *alone* "apart from works prescribed by the law." Since Paul obviously contrasts "faith" with "works prescribed by the law," saying that a person is justified by the one and not the other, Luther's addition of the word *alone* doesn't seem like much of a stretch. Other important Christian commentators had explained Romans 3:28 using the Latin phrase *sola fide,* "faith alone." The difference, however, is in what Luther meant by the essential terms *justification, faith,* and *works.* Prior to Luther, faith was assumed to include living a morally upright life. A person of faith could be identified by acts of Christian piety and charity; a person was judged faithful by the kind of life he or she led. By contrast, for Luther faith referred to something that excluded works. Moreover, for him faith meant something precise and relatively narrow: Having faith meant having faith *in* Jesus. And having faith in Jesus was the only thing necessary for salvation.

# FAITH *IN* JESUS CHRIST, FAITH *OF* JESUS CHRIST

This brings us to another of Luther's highly influential translation decisions. In Romans, he translated the Greek phrases *pistis Iesou Christou* (3:22) and *pistis Iesou* (3:26) in a way that removed a long-recognized ambiguity about whether the sense of the language meant "faith *of* Jesus Christ" or "faith *in* Jesus Christ." Luther rendered the phrases so they would unequivocally read "faith *in* Jesus Christ." In the centuries following Luther, Protestant readers assumed that when Paul speaks of being justified by faith, he means faith in Christ. But among Pauline scholars today, the debate about how to translate *pistis Iesou Christou* is on-going. The theological implications of how this phrase is translated are enormous—and worth a brief lesson in Greek grammar.

Like German and Latin, Greek uses special word endings to indicate whether a word is the subject, object, or indirect object of a sentence. Rather than relying on word order, as in English, the Greek language changes the form of the noun, usually by adding an ending. The Greek phrase *pistis Iesou* (in 3:26) is literally two nouns side by side; *pistis* is the word for "faith"; *Iesou* is the word for "Jesus." In English, a preposition is required in order to make sense of how these two words relate to each other. Virtually all English Bibles use "in" for the phrase *pistis Iesou,* hence rendering it "faith in Jesus." But a significant number of scholars have argued that "faith *of* Jesus" is the better translation. That is why the NRSV has a note in Romans 3:22 and 26 indicating "faith of Jesus Christ" and "faith of Jesus" as alternative translations.

Choosing the preposition *in* to accompany the name *Iesou* is to interpret the phrase so that "Jesus" is the object of "faith"; and the subject—human believers—is not stated but implied. On the other hand, to read the phrase as "faith *of* Jesus" is to see Jesus as the subject, not the object of faith. "Faith of Jesus" then would refer to Jesus' own faith. It is fascinating but somewhat disconcerting to think that such a profound point of theology can hinge upon the specificity of Luther's German or the ambiguity of Paul's Greek.

As is always true of language and communication, though, context makes all the difference in clearing a path to understanding. The best way to judge whether Paul means faith *in* or faith *of* is to take into consideration the larger context of Romans and Paul's theology in general. Consider: There is no place in Romans where Paul defines, describes, or in any other way explicitly articulates the ideal expression of religious faith as having faith in Jesus. Whenever Paul specifies the direction toward which human faith should be focused, it is always toward God. And he makes this unambiguously clear by using the appropriate prepositions. Reading *pistis Iesou Christou* as "faith of Jesus Christ" means that the object of Christ's faith, while not specified here, is none other than God. If indeed Romans is a text about God, then translating this ambiguous phrase as "faith *of* Christ" is surely consistent with Paul's thinking in Romans.

> There is no place in Romans where Paul defines, describes, or in any other way explicitly articulates the ideal expression of religious faith as having faith in Jesus. Whenever Paul specifies the direction toward which human faith should be focused, it is always toward God.

# INVITATION TO DISCIPLESHIP

Due in large part to Augustine's reading of Romans 1–3, we regard human nature as inherently evil or inevitably sinful. As a result, we face God's condemnation with no hope of doing anything ourselves to bridge the gap between God's righteousness and our sinfulness. And while each of us may have the capacity to do good or evil, we are held accountable to the law of God yet not made righteous by that law. Only through God's intervention and grace can we be justified and be made righteous. But if we take Paul at his word in Romans 2:12-16, then in the end we see that good works *do* count for something in God's economy, even if they cannot save us. Although we cannot make ourselves righteous in God's eyes, we can and should live as righteous a life as we are capable of, precisely because God holds us all up to the same standard. In other words, we live (as righteously as we can) by faith. "Do we then overthrow the law by this faith? By no means! On the contrary, we uphold the law" (Romans 3:31).

And while we're on the subject of faith, consider the implications of reading Romans 3:22 as "faith *in* Jesus Christ" or as "faith *of* Jesus Christ." Does it matter in terms of our own faith how we read that phrase? Perhaps. If we prefer the objective reading (faith *in* Jesus), then we place an emphasis on our own efforts to claim and faithfully follow Jesus as Lord as the means by which we are saved. If we prefer the subjective reading (faith *of* Jesus), then we place an emphasis on Jesus' own efforts to fulfill his role faithfully as God's Messiah as the means by which we are saved. What is at stake is how we respond to Paul's invitation to participate in Jesus' own faith in God. Perhaps, then, we should even consider seeing the phrase *pistis Iesou* as both objective and subjective, calling us to be faithful to God through our belief in Jesus as well as to imitate Jesus' way of being faithful to God. The ultimate direction in which our faith—and Christ's own faith—is headed is toward God, the only one who is righteous.

# FOR REFLECTION

- What is your understanding of human nature? What is your understanding of the doctrine of original sin? How does seeing humans as made in the image of God fit into your understanding of human nature and original sin?

- What is the correlation between justification and the righteousness of God?

- How would you describe a person of faith? How would you explain the difference in reading Romans 3:22 as referring to the "faith *of* Jesus Christ" or "faith *in* Jesus Christ?" Which reading do you support and why?

# Abraham, Father of All

*For what does the scripture say? "Abraham believed God, and it was reckoned to him as righteousness."*

—Romans 4:3

## INTRODUCTION

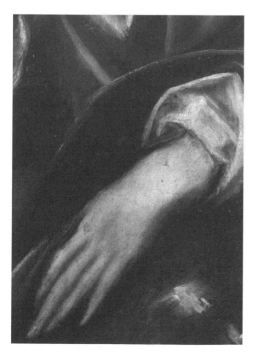

Abraham figures prominently in two of Paul's letters: Romans and Galatians. There is a great deal of overlap between the two letters in terms of what Paul has to say about Abraham. In both of them, he basically quotes Genesis 15:6: "Abraham believed God, and it was reckoned to him as righteousness." Then he proceeds to explain the verse in light of other verses from Scripture. In both letters, Paul uses the language of Genesis 15:6 to support the phrase so often associated with his name: *justification by faith.*

Traditionally, interpreters of Romans have understood Abraham to function as Paul's premier illustration of justification by faith. First, Abraham is lifted up as an example of the kind of faith one should have in God and the way in which God responds to such faith. In other words,

39

Paul invokes Abraham in order to inspire others to have the same kind of faith the great patriarch had. Second, the story of Abraham is taken to be a proof for the validity of the doctrine of justification by faith. God reckons Abraham righteous by virtue of nothing more than his faith.

More recent interpreters have stressed the significance of Abraham as a founding father for Paul. Abraham is the first in a line of descendants counted as the people of God. And as God says to the people over and over in the Old Testament, God will not abandon them for the sake of his promise to Abraham. According to this line of interpretation, Paul appeals to Abraham in order to show that the Gentiles have the right to claim Abraham as their father just as much as the Jews. The relationship of justification by faith to Abraham in Romans 3–4 remains important for understanding Paul's discussion in this section of Romans.

# DAILY ASSIGNMENTS

As you read this week's selection of texts, all of which relate to Abraham in some way, reflect on the way the themes of God's righteousness and justification by faith—themes prominent in Romans 1–3—relate to Paul's discussion of Abraham in Romans 4.

## DAY ONE: Genesis 15–16

In Romans and Galatians, Paul places great emphasis on Genesis 15:6, where Abraham is said to be reckoned righteous because of his faith. How do these chapters from Genesis provide context for Paul's quotation of Genesis 15:6 and his interpretation of that verse?

## DAY TWO: Genesis 17:1–18:15; 21:1-21

These additional chapters from Genesis continue Abraham's story, focusing especially on the birth of Isaac. Pay particular attention to the theme of promise and fulfillment.

## DAY THREE: Romans 4:1–5:11

How does Paul's emphasis on faith and justification relate to the theme of promise and fulfillment, and how do both relate to Abraham's story?

## DAY FOUR: Galatians 3:6–4:7

How would you compare Paul's interpretation of Genesis 15:6 and his treatment of Abraham in Galatians to what he says about Abraham in Romans 4?

## DAY FIVE: Commentary

Read the commentary in the participant book.

## DAY SIX: Romans 4:1–5:11

Reread the week's selection from Romans in light of the other assigned texts and the commentary.

# ABRAHAM IN ANCIENT JUDAISM

The story of Abraham comprises a large chunk of Genesis and is an integral part of the narrative, which recounts the origins of humanity and the formation of God's people. Abraham's story, though, also stands as an independent epic with an endearing and all-too-human hero at its center—a hero to Jews as well as to Christians and Muslims.

In Genesis, Abraham is portrayed as the ancestral patriarch of the Jews, the "founding father" of the Jewish people. Because of this special stature, he came to be regarded as a figure representative of the Jewish people generally. With the possible exception of Moses, Abraham held unrivaled status as the most important figure in the history of Israel. Much as legends about George Washington reflect what it meant to be American, Abraham's biography was taken as representative of what it meant to be Jewish, both in terms of virtues to which individual Jews aspired and in terms of what it meant to be part of the people called Israel.

By Paul's time, stories about Abraham went far beyond the patriarch's biblical biography. Various retellings of the Abraham story are found among the numerous **extra-canonical Jewish writings** preserved from antiquity, many of which are dated within a century or two of Paul. Post-biblical Abraham stories tend to illustrate particular virtues traditionally associated with Abraham, the most prominent being Abraham's legendary faith.

**Extra-canonical Jewish writings that explain or expand the Genesis accounts of Abraham include: (1) the Testament of Abraham, an entertaining ancient novel that recounts how Abraham died; (2) the Genesis Apocryphon, an Aramaic manuscript discovered among the Dead Sea Scrolls that retells portions of the patriarchal narratives; and (3) the Book of Jubilees, a second-century B.C. Hebrew text that retells the stories from Genesis 1 through Exodus 20.**

The image of Abraham as God's most faithful servant combined with his image as the founding father of Israel led to a widespread tradition that he was the first monotheist in human history. In other words, he became known as the first person to recognize—and subsequently put his faith in—the one and only living God. Many ancient interpreters of the biblical story were no doubt struck by the abruptness of God's call of the patriarch, as well as by Abraham's equally abrupt willingness to leave kin and country in response to a God heretofore unknown (Genesis 12:1-4). Not surprisingly, stories developed that helped to fill in the gaps about how the relationship between God and Abraham got started. In these stories, Abraham is a skilled astronomer who spends a lot of time gazing at the stars. (Abraham was a Chaldean, and the Chaldeans were famous for their prowess in astronomy.) Eventually, his meditations of the heavens lead him to the realization that there must be a celestial superpower in charge of the universe.

In the Greco-Roman period, monotheism came to be regarded as practically synonymous with Judaism—by Greeks as well as Jews. The stories about Abraham had the advantage both of explaining how and why Abraham came to be the father of the Jewish people and of crediting the Jews' ancestral figure with making the all-important discovery of God. One interesting side effect of this emphasis on Abraham as the first person to recognize the one God is that it requires Abraham to have been something other than a Jew to start with. Israel was obviously not yet constituted as a nation during Abraham's lifetime. In other words, he was not an Israelite by birth, as the Genesis story makes clear. That makes him, as Hellenistic Jews noted, the first proselyte—that is, the first convert to Judaism. Therefore, his identity encompassed both Jew and Gentile. Besides, God's promise to Abraham was not simply that the patriarch would be the father of *a* great nation but rather a *multitude* of nations (Genesis 17:4; Greek: *ethne*). So when Paul argues that Abraham is the father of Gentiles as well as Jews, he is relying on a legitimate reading of Scripture while also drawing on popular Jewish tradition of his day.

# TWO READINGS OF ABRAHAM IN ROMANS 4

As we saw with Romans 1–3, there is more than one way to read Romans 4. Consider the question posed in 4:1: According to the way it is typically translated in the NRSV, the question reads, "What then are we to say was gained by Abraham, our ancestor according to the flesh?" Reading the question this way signals that Paul will address the issue of faith versus works. Did Abraham merit what he gained, or was it granted to him by God's grace? Was Abraham justified by works or by faith? The answer, of course, is that Abraham was justified by faith; Genesis 15:6 is proof of that. Because Abraham was deemed righteous before he was circumcised, he could not have earned his righteousness; it was simply bestowed on him as a gift. Thus, the purpose of Paul's appeal to Abraham is to prove that God justifies people not by their works but by their faith and that others may be inspired to follow the example of Abraham's faith.

But wait. This interpretation doesn't really take into account much of anything Paul says after Romans 4:10—not even half-way through the chapter! Yet the latter half of Romans 4 is the critical component of Paul's argument, namely that Abraham is the father of Jews and Gentiles, the father of all who show faith in the one, true, living God.

So consider another way to translate Romans 4:1: "What then shall we say? Have we found Abraham to be our ancestor according to the flesh?" (Eisenbaum's translation). Read this way, the question asks who has the right to call Abraham "father" and thus stake a claim on the inheritance promised to Abraham's heirs. There are good grammatical reasons to support the alternative translation, but the contextual reasons are more important. If we look at Romans 4 in its entirety, Paul's discussion emphasizes Abraham's role as ancestor. The chapter culminates recalling how Abraham's trust in God's promise concerning Isaac inaugurates a divinely blessed line of descendants (4:16-21). The significant point about Abraham's faith in Romans 4 is not that he acknowledged the existence of the Creator God—although that was important for initiating the relationship between God and Abraham—but that he demonstrated his faith in God's promises by conceiving Isaac. Abraham acted in such a way as to enable the realization of God's promises. Without Abraham's cooperation, the promise of Isaac could not have been fulfilled. We could say that Abraham had faith in the faithfulness of God—faith that God makes good on God's promises, even when one has to wait a very

> Abraham had faith in the faithfulness of God— faith that God makes good on God's promises, even when one has to wait a very long time to see them fulfilled.

long time to see them fulfilled. Underlying Paul's repeated emphasis on God's promise to Abraham is a theology that puts great stock in the integrity of God.

So when Paul asks, "Have we found Abraham to be our ancestor according to the flesh?" the answer is "Absolutely not!" Abraham is the ancestor of God's people according to the promise. After all, if being a descendant of Abraham were contingent upon "flesh," then the birth of Ishmael would have been sufficient to fulfill the divine promise. But God's promise to make Abraham "exceedingly fruitful" (Genesis 17:6) is not fulfilled until the birth of Isaac—when Abraham is 110 years old! In other words, physical descent was never what made a Jew part of Abraham's lineage. Surely then it is not necessary for Gentiles either, especially because God's promise to Abraham is that he will be "the father of many nations," as Paul reminds us in Romans 4:18 (remember, "nations" may also be translated "Gentiles").

# JUSTIFICATION BY FAITH

To say that justification by faith means one is justified by one's faith in Jesus (and further that Jesus is the only means of justification) belies an understanding rooted in the traditional reading of Romans 3:21-26. As we discerned earlier in Session 2 (pages 34–35), verses 22 and 26 are often interpreted to mean that justification comes through faith *in* Christ. A problem arises when Paul's discussion of Abraham in Romans 4 is then taken as proof of this claim; for the object of Abraham's faith could not have been Jesus, since the patriarch lived long before the time of Jesus. So who or what then *is* the object of Abraham's faith? God, of course. That means it is Abraham's *faith in God* that brings justification: "He believed the LORD; and the LORD reckoned it to him as righteousness" (Genesis 15:6). In other words, in Abraham's case, Christ does not figure in the justification by faith equation.

But what if we interpret the significance of Romans 4 to be not about how Abraham as an individual became justified but rather how *others* become justified because of what Abraham did? In this reading, the faith of Abraham (4:16; *pistis Abraham*) works in a way similar to the faith of Jesus (3:26; *pistis Iesou*). The faith of both bestows benefits on others. Abraham helped fulfill God's promise that he would become the "father of many nations." He gave birth to the people of God, who are not constituted only of Jews but also of all those who believe in God, Jew and Gentile alike. In the same way, Jesus' central act of faithfulness was obedience unto death, a sacrifice great enough to atone for the sins of all those whose sins had previously been passed over (Romans 3:25)—that is, the Gentiles.

**Justification by faith is Paul's way of expressing the role of God's grace in the scheme of salvation.**

Therefore, justification by faith is Paul's way of expressing the role of God's grace in the scheme of salvation. God works in concert with certain individuals to guide creation toward God's intended purposes. While the traditional interpretation sees a person's faith in Christ as granting justification and therefore salvation, this other interpretation sees the faithful action(s) of one person—specially charged with carrying out the divine will—as attaining justification and therefore salvation for the many. The traditional reading reflects an individualistic understanding of salvation; the other reading reflects a collective understanding. Grace plays a role in both. But the key difference is in how grace functions. The traditional way (championed by Luther) views grace as primarily functioning to remind people that they are not deserving of salvation because of their wretched, sinful nature. The other way views grace as functioning quite literally as a gift from God; for the children of Abraham are now the beneficiaries of the blessings promised to Abraham, not because of their own merit but because of Abraham's merit, on account of the patriarch's great faith.

Paul's ultimate point in this section is that through Christ's death, the promise that Abraham would be the father of many nations has been realized (Galatians 3:28-29). Gentiles may now claim Abraham as their father, which means they are entitled to the same divine favor that Israel has already enjoyed. As God frequently reminds the Israelites throughout the Old Testament, because of the blessings God promised Abraham and his descendants, God never abandons Israel (though God sometimes "hides his face" in response to Israel's unfaithfulness). To be a child of Abraham is to be a favored child of God. To be justified by faith, therefore, means first of all that the nations have been justified by Christ's faith, not their own faith; and secondly, it means that Gentiles now have a share in the eternal blessings God promised to Abraham. It is through the faith *of* Christ (in God) that Abraham's children are now reckoned righteous in God's sight.

# INVITATION TO DISCIPLESHIP

Paul uses Abraham to illuminate his message to the Romans in at least three ways.

(1) By lifting up the example of Abraham, Paul points out characteristics believers should have in their own experiences of faith. Just as Abraham trusted in God even though his situation seemed hopeless and barren, we too are challenged to respond to similar times of crisis and trial with a similar kind of trust; for it is at times like these—perhaps most especially—that we experience God's grace. It is at times like these that we turn things over to God and God's grace intervenes, and all that is required from us is acceptance.

(2) Paul also takes the story of Abraham as proof of the believer's justification by faith alone. Just as God "reckoned" to Abraham righteousness, so God reckons to us the same righteousness. What God does on our behalf is made apparent by what we cannot do to merit God's action. We are made right with God on the basis of nothing other than our trust in God.

(3) Paul appeals to Abraham in order to show that Gentiles have the right to claim Abraham as their father just as much as Jews do. Furthermore, it is through both the faithfulness of Abraham and the faithfulness of Jesus that all of creation is to be guided toward God's intended purpose. Through Abraham's obedience in life, literally fathering the first generation of the Jews, the people of God were born. Through Jesus' obedience unto death, the Gentiles were justified.

In light of the example of Abraham Paul gives, we should see our faith in God as aimed to carry out God's intended purpose, not merely for ourselves but for all people and for all of creation.

# FOR REFLECTION

• What characteristics in Abraham's life do you feel are crucial for a life of faith?

• Read Romans 4:19-21. What makes you fully convinced God will do what God promises?

• In the context of the cultural and religious struggles in our world today, what are the implications of Paul's insistence that Abraham is father of us all? What does it mean for Christians to call themselves children of Abraham today?

# Christic, the New Adam

*Therefore just as one man's trespass led to condemnation for all,
so one man's act of righteousness leads to justification
and life for all.*

—Romans 5:18

## INTRODUCTION

Once again, Paul turns to Scripture to assist him in making his case. In Romans 4, he devotes considerable attention to Abraham, the ancestral patriarch of Israel. In Romans 5, he turns his attention to Adam, the primal ancestor of the human race. Although many interpreters assume the story of the Fall is the foundation underlying everything Paul has said since Romans 1, his first actual appeal to the garden of Eden story occurs when he compares Christ to Adam in Romans 5. And compared to the first four chapters of Romans, in which Christ is mentioned infrequently, in Romans 5–8 Paul's real interest is in explaining the significance of Christ.

Paul compares Adam and Christ in two of his letters, here in Romans 5 and also in 1 Corinthians 15. Some of the same themes appear in both comparisons: baptism, death, resurrection, and eternal life. But the overall thrust of each discussion is markedly different. In 1 Corinthians 15, Paul is keen to emphasize the validity and nature of the impending resurrection of believers, presumably against some at Corinth, who say there is no resurrection of the dead. The comparison between Adam and Christ in 1 Corinthians 15 serves to demonstrate the way human beings will partake of Christ's nature in the world to come (immortality) just as they partake of Adam's nature in this world (mortality). In Romans 5, sin is the critical issue rather than the nature of resurrection. "For just as by the one man's disobedience the many were made sinners, so by the one man's obedience the many will be made righteous" (5:19). In other words, in Romans 5, Paul is concerned with believers' fundamental ethical orientation as human beings who straddle two realms of existence—one connected to Adam and one connected to Christ.

# DAILY ASSIGNMENTS

In this week's reading, pay attention to the similarities and differences between Adam and Jesus as well as the different qualities of Christ that Paul tends to emphasize in various contexts.

## DAY ONE: Genesis 2–3

As you read the familiar story about the garden of Eden, look for any details you may never have noticed before.

## DAY TWO: Romans 5:12–6:14

How would you describe Paul's analogy between Adam and Christ?

## DAY THREE: 1 Corinthians 15

How does the analogy between Adam and Christ in 1 Corinthians 15 differ from the one in Romans 5?

## DAY FOUR: Philippians 2:1-18

This text contains one of the oldest surviving ancient Christian hymns. Look for connections between the portrait of Jesus in this text and the one Paul describes when comparing him to Adam in Romans 5.

## DAY FIVE: Commentary

Read the commentary in the participant book.

## DAY SIX: Romans 5:12–6:14

Reread the week's selection from Romans in light of the other assigned texts and the commentary.

# ADAM, SIN, AND DEATH

Compared to Abraham, Moses, and David, there is little reflection on the figure of Adam in Old Testament Scripture outside the garden of Eden story itself. Christian interpreters of the third and fourth centuries (and beyond) reflect a great deal on the story of Adam and Eve, writing volumes of commentary on the primeval history of Genesis. The few references to Adam in Jewish texts written close to Paul's time comment on the connection between Adam, sin, and mortality. For example, in a work known as Second Esdras, parts of which had canonical or semi-canonical status in some Christian circles, the creation of Adam is recalled in a vision—how God "breathed into him the breath of life, and he was made alive in [God's] presence." But Adam's demise is quickly recalled as well: "And you laid upon him one commandment of yours; but he transgressed it, and immediately you appointed death for him and for his descendants" (2 Esdras 3:7).

We read in Genesis how God places Adam in the garden of Eden and tells him he may eat of every tree, with one exception: the tree of the knowledge of good and evil. Of that tree, "you shall not eat," God says to Adam, "for in the day that you eat of it you shall die" (Genesis 2:17). These words form the very first commandment. Not only is Genesis 2:17 the first divine ethical imperative, it also comes with the threat of punishment: Eat of the tree, and the punishment is death.

> "Through his [Adam's] sin he subjected his descendants to the punishment of sin and damnation, for he had radically corrupted them, in himself, by his sinning. As a consequence of this, all those descended from him and his wife...all these entered into the inheritance of original sin."[3]
> (*Augustine*)

And so the story goes. Eve is strolling through the garden one day when the serpent comes along and persuades her to eat from the forbidden tree. She then persuades her husband to eat from the tree. The transgression leads to their expulsion from the garden. This first act of disobedience eventually becomes known as the "original sin" that leads to the fall of humankind. That moment initiates an ever-widening chasm between the human and divine realm, or so seems to be the conventional understanding. The rest of Old Testament Scripture is generally read as the story of ever-increasing disobedience, making abundantly clear the need for salvation, which must come from a divine source since human beings of every generation continue to rebel against God.

But this understanding of the garden of Eden story comes to us today laden with centuries of reflection since the coming of Christ and the subsequent success of Christianity. Paul, on the other hand, looks to Adam to illumine the significance of Christ without all those centuries of reflection. He reads Genesis without knowing what Augustine will say, or Dante, or Milton, or Martin Luther for that matter. In other words, Paul stands at the beginning of what will eventually become the enormous accumulated tradition of interpretation on the first three chapters of Genesis. And from that vantage point, what Paul sees is the age of Adam coming to an end very soon.

Thus, in Romans 5, Paul is not trying to make the point that the beginning of all human history already pointed to the cosmic necessity of a savior. For Paul and his contemporaries, the garden of Eden was not taken as a story about the hopelessly sinful nature of human beings. Most first-century readers saw it as a tragic tale that explained why human beings die. Although the text of Genesis itself is ambiguous about whether Adam and Eve were originally created immortal, Hellenistic Jewish interpreters similar to Paul saw the story linking mortality to sin and corruption, and immortality to righteousness and goodness (for example, see Wisdom of Solomon 2:23-24).

Perhaps human mortality required conscious reflection for Jews of antiquity—more so than for others—because the notion that humans are created in the image of God was central to the Jewish understanding of humanity and the relationship between humans and God. But immortality was the fundamental quality in ancient mythology that distinguished divinity from humanity. In Greek tradition, the gods are commonly known as "immortals." The God of Israel, too, was assumed to be immortal. What does it mean then to say that humans are created in the image of God? Surely this question looms large as Paul compares Adam and Christ and the way in which they represent two versions of what it means to be created in the image of God.

# THE ONE AND THE MANY, THE MANY AND THE ALL

The traditional interpretation of Romans 5 is rooted in Augustine's doctrine of original sin, and not surprisingly, Augustine grounded his notion of original sin in his interpretation of Romans 5. According to Augustine, Romans 5:12 meant that sin—and consequently death—spreads to each and every human being like a gene that passes from one generation to the next. This understanding of original sin led to the inconvenient but nevertheless logical conclusion that unbaptized infants are not innocents but rather unredeemed sinners. Although **Augustine's theological opponents (Pelagius, for example)** vigorously disputed the notion that newborns could seriously be considered sinners, Augustine's view eventually won out. Original sin became a doctrine entrenched in Western Christian thought. Even though many Protestants later rejected the Augustinian doctrine of original sin, the concept of human nature as inherently sinful was retained and even emphasized. Many of the Protestant Reformers stressed the depravity of humanity in their teaching and preaching, more so than had been prevalent in European Catholicism prior to the Reformation. The same attitude informed American Puritanism in the Colonial period and still finds voice in certain expressions of Christianity today.

"Righteousness had more power in bringing to life than sin in putting to death, because Adam killed only himself and his own descendants, but Christ freed both those who at that time were in the body and the following generations."[4]
(*Pelagius*)

This understanding of human nature as inherently sinful is closely linked with the traditional understanding of justification by faith. If one views sin as an inevitable part of being human, then humans are incapable of making the moral progress necessary for attaining justification and thus salvation. And if they cannot work their way to salvation, all humans can do is have faith—in traditional Christian terms, faith *in* Jesus Christ, whose death atones for their sins, thereby crediting to them the righteousness necessary for salvation. But as we reasoned earlier, if we view being justified by faith to mean that one is justified by the faith *of* Christ, not by one's own faith, then Jesus' faithfulness affects—or potentially affects—all of humanity, whether or not individual humans believe in Jesus. From this viewpoint, the way Jesus' actions affect humans would then more closely parallel the way Adam's actions affected humans.

Most of what Paul has to say in his comparison of Adam and Christ is how Christ undid the damage caused by Adam. "The free gift is not like the trespass" (5:15). Interpreters today reading Romans 5 point out that the primary similarity between Adam and Christ (according to Paul) is how the actions of the one affect the many. However, this view differs from the Augustinian understanding, in which all who are "in Adam" are hopelessly sinful and thus condemned, while all who are "in Christ" are justified and therefore saved. According to the Augustinian view, all human beings are condemnable sinners because of Adam, apart from their own moral action, and all human beings "in Christ" are similarly saved, that is to say, also apart from their own moral action (but not apart from the requirement of faith).

But just as we observed in Romans 2, Paul is very much concerned with the moral caliber of those who claim to be among the people of God. Morality is hardly irrelevant to Paul's argument: "Should we continue in sin in order that grace may abound?" (6:1). Indeed, the ethical exhortations that characterize Romans 6—"Do not let sin exercise dominion in your mortal bodies" (6:12)— follow as the practical implications drawn from the discussion about Adam and Christ in Romans 5.

For Paul, to be "in" or "of" Adam means to be both a descendant of Adam and to be similar to him. In Paul's cultural context, being a descendant of a certain ancestor implied you were also like him (or sometimes her). In a modern context, we assume somewhat less linkage of this sort yet still acknowledge some overlap between our family heritage and our behavior. For example, any adult charged with a crime stands before the law solely accountable for his or her actions. Yet in some cases, it is reasonable to appeal to a person's background or environment in assigning blame. Deciding to what extent such environmental factors make individuals less accountable for their actions is a difficult matter, but such factors may sometimes be regarded as mitigating circumstances.

In short, although modern American society in theory holds individuals accountable for wrongs they have committed, it also recognizes that the "sins of the fathers" sometimes really are visited upon the children. Conversely, individual accomplishments in our culture are generally credited to the individual's talent and effort, but a person may have benefited from advantages provided by his or her parents. In other words, just as the sins of the fathers are visited upon some children, the "blessings of the fathers" are visited upon others. In either case, the actions of the one can affect the lives of the many in lasting and powerful ways.

The question about how the one relates to the many—and especially *how far* the actions of the one extend—has nowhere been more seriously contemplated than in Romans 5:18. Here, Paul articulates a rather strong symmetrical parallelism between Adam and Christ: "Therefore just as one man's trespass led to condemnation for *all*, so one man's act of righteousness leads to justification and life for *all*" (italics added for emphasis). Some Christian interpreters recognized that this verse had the potential to be read as making a claim for universal salvation, because Paul seems to say that the saving effect of Christ's obedience will extend as far as Adam's act of disobedience did—that is, to all of humanity. **Origen is probably the most famous Christian commentator to have argued for a vision of salvation that included all of creation**—not only all human beings but also devils and demons! (Of course, Origen's view of universal salvation was also condemned as heresy.)

"We think, indeed, that the goodness of God, through His Christ, may recall all His creatures to one end, even His enemies being conquered and subdued.... Whether any of these orders who act under the government of the devil, and obey his wicked commands, will in a future world be converted to righteousness because of their possessing the faculty of freedom of will...is a result which you yourself, reader, may approve of."[5]
*(Origen)*

Most Christian interpreters dismiss the possibility that Paul meant universal salvation. For example, Thomas Aquinas and Martin Luther argued that every human being is physically born of Adam, but not every human being is born of Christ.[6] Thus, while the first "all" in Romans 5:18 refers to every human being, the second "all" refers only to those who have been spiritually reborn in Christ through baptism.

However, the inability to conceive that *Paul* would imagine the salvation of all humankind once again derives more from later Christian doctrine than from Romans. Surely for Paul, Christ's act of faithfulness cannot be less powerful than Adam's act of disobedience. To the contrary, Paul asserts in Romans 5:15 that the free gift wrought by Christ *is* of greater magnitude than the consequence of the trespass wrought by Adam. Paul sees Christ as the one who inaugurates the new age, the age of redemption. He is the firstborn of God's children, and in this sense Christ is truly a new Adam. But this new Adam heralds the age of peace, righteousness, and immortality while simultaneously marking the end of the age of strife, corruption, and death.

# INVITATION TO DISCIPLESHIP

One way to approach this week's readings in Romans is to ask, What does it mean to say that humans are created in the image of God? According to Paul in Romans 5, there are two ways to answer that question. One way is to look at Adam; the other way is to look at Christ. Looking at Adam (and Eve), we see God's good creation as it was intended to be until, by a single act of disobedience (under a tree), sin and death entered into the picture. Looking at Christ, on the other hand, we see God's good creation restored by a single act of obedience (on a cross), whereby sin and death no longer dominate the scene. Thus, to see ourselves in Adam is to lament our own disobedience and ultimate mortality; and to see ourselves in Christ is to celebrate the gift of God's righteousness and the promise of eternal life.

Another way to approach this week's readings is to ask, How do the actions of the one (Adam or Christ) affect the many? According to Paul, Adam's act brings condemnation and death to all; Christ's act brings justification and life to all. What's more, Christ's one act has greater impact on us all than Adam's one act ever had (Romans 5:15). That very notion should give us pause. Perhaps we should examine carefully our traditional understanding of original sin to be sure we do not focus more on our sinfulness than we do on God's grace. Perhaps we should consider the scope of God's salvation to be sure we ourselves do not count some people out of the new age to come. And perhaps we should be sure "the abundance of grace" (Romans 5:17b) does not become a rationale for making little or no effort in presenting ourselves to God as "instruments of righteousness" (6:13).

# FOR REFLECTION

- Describe in your own words how Adam and Christ represent two versions of what it means to be created in the image of God.

- Think of examples where the actions of one individual have influenced the lives of many. Where do you see the action of Adam (disobedience) and the action of Christ (obedience) exemplified in the world?

- How do you understand what Paul says in Romans 5:18? What are your thoughts regarding universal salvation? How does this view fit (or not fit) into your image of God? How does this view fit (or not fit) into your image of humanity?

# Sin, Law, and Grace

*For sin, seizing an opportunity in the commandment,
deceived me and through it killed me. So the law is holy,
and the commandment is holy and just and good.*

—Romans 7:11-12

## INTRODUCTION

We are about to enter some of the most convoluted material in Paul's writings and perhaps in the entire Bible: Romans 7. Not surprisingly, it is also one of the most notoriously debated. Part of the problem lies with the way the apostle communicates. Paul seems to speak with more than one voice in Romans 7. It feels to modern readers as if he is carrying on a schizophrenic conversation with himself about the value of the "law." On the one hand, Paul says sinful passions are aroused by the law, and at some points he even seems to imply that the law causes sin (7:5, 8-11). On the other hand, Paul proclaims the law holy, just, and good (7:12) as well as spiritual (7:14). This other voice implies that sin acts independently of law and in opposition to it.

59

Generally speaking, it seems only reasonable to assume Paul would not intentionally contradict himself. Statements that appear as contradictions must be treated with patience, benevolence, and humility. What appears as a contradiction on the surface can, on closer scrutiny, be explained as part of a coherent argument more nuanced and complicated than we might at first realize. We can eventually come to a better understanding of Paul's view of the law if we make a concerted effort to listen carefully and pay attention to rhetorical and contextual clues.

# DAILY ASSIGNMENTS

Here in the mid-section of Romans, it can be extremely challenging to follow the flow of Paul's teaching. If ever there was a time to read slowly and carefully and to reread the texts several times over, this is it! Allow yourself the opportunity to note any passages you find particularly difficult to comprehend. And as suggested earlier, don't pass too quickly over any passage that is familiar. Ask yourself if you really understand what it means.

## DAY ONE: Psalm 119:1-40, 113-144

The psalmist extols the virtue of God's law; faithful adherence to it, along with diligent reflection on its teachings, is the primary means of properly relating to God and of exercising justice within the human community.

## DAY TWO: Romans 6:15–7:6

Note any similarities of language and subject matter that you see in this section of Romans and Chapter 1.

## DAY THREE: Romans 7:7–8:17

The typical cause of confusion to readers of Romans 7 is that Paul appears to be of "two minds" in describing the relationship between law and sin. See if you can articulate in your own words what Paul is saying about law and sin while noting any statements that don't seem to fit your description.

## DAY FOUR: Galatians 4:21–5:26

Many interpreters think Paul's view of the law is more negative in Galatians than Romans. Do you think that is true? Or does Galatians seem to reflect the same essential attitude, just in a different context?

## DAY FIVE: Commentary

Read the commentary in the participant book.

## DAY SIX: Romans 6:15–8:17

Reread the week's selection from Romans in light of the other assigned texts and the commentary.

# "WRETCHED MAN THAT I AM!"

It is essential for understanding Romans 7 that we consider the identity of the person who begins speaking in verse 7. Paul shifts from speaking in the first common plural voice of "we" (7:7a) to speaking in the singular "I" (*ego* in Greek), with pointed emphasis (7:7b). It has been assumed for centuries that in Romans 7:7-25, Paul is speaking of his personal experience. More specifically, he is speaking of his personal spiritual development—how he realized the intractable nature of sin as it characterizes human life and how the law does not so much mitigate sin as magnify the problem of sin. Paul expresses his awareness of sin as a problem and ultimately explains how he recognized the futility of human moral striving against the power of sin and the necessity of salvation by means of Christ. As we read about Paul speaking of his own religious experience in particular, we assume he is talking about human experience in general, though from the perspective of a Jew-turned-Christian believer.

This orientation to Romans 7:7-25 can be traced back to Augustine. Although he interpreted this passage differently at various points in his life, he eventually settled on taking it to be the apostle's autobiographical reflections. The assumption that Paul is speaking of his own conversion has been the "default" reading of this text until very recently.

The Latin phrase *simul iustus et peccator*, meaning "at the same time justified and a sinner," summarizes Martin Luther's description of the Christian's state after conversion: "The saints in being righteous are at the same time sinners; they are righteous because they believe in Christ whose righteousness covers them..., but they are sinners because they do not fulfill the law."[7]
(*Martin Luther*)

Furthermore, Augustine became convinced that the internal struggle represented by the divided self that speaks in these verses represents the ongoing struggle of every Christian. Martin Luther followed Augustine and saw Romans 7 as the fundamental underpinning of his famous Latin slogan *simul iustus et peccator*, "at the same time justified and a sinner." This traditional reading of Romans 7 thus explains the conflicting statements about law as reflecting a person's internal dialogue, which in turn reflects the conflict human beings experience between what God wants, which is pure and good, and what human nature desires, which is sin. As we have already discussed, Luther, Calvin, and other Protestant Reformers had an extremely pessimistic understanding of human nature. Even though Christians are justified by their faith in Christ, they remain unchanged sinners. Baptism in Christ enables believers to belong to the body of Christ without being morally transformed. The "transformation" lies in the recognition of their total dependence on God's grace, along with the realization that there is nothing they can do to become better in God's sight. Of course, recognition of God's grace can only be realized by baptism and conversion to Christianity. According to this traditional interpretation, the real difference between "before" and "after" is that we now have hope of salvation in spite of our wretched condition. Therefore, conversion constitutes a personal, interior insight and embrace of divine grace, experienced as a form of spiritual acceptance and accompanied by a feeling of psychological calm. Romans 7:7-25 was taken to be the description of Paul's very own experience of conversion, which became a model for future Christian conversions.

But before Augustine, Christian interpreters saw problems with an autobiographical reading of Romans 7:7-25. Early Christian theologians knew that sometimes a speaker assumes the voice of an imagined other in order to provide a different vantage point on the topic at hand. (This is what is known as *prosopopeia,* or speech-in-character; it was a rather common rhetorical device in antiquity.) They—and later Augustine—also recognized that Paul regularly employed this kind of rhetoric. Unfortunately, it is not commonly used today and thus is practically impossible for modern readers to spot. However, recent commentators on Romans now acknowledge that Paul is using speech-in-character in Chapter 7, but they differ about the identity of the character(s) whose voice Paul assumes.

> *prosopopeia*
> (Greek: *prosopopoiia*):
> According to *The American Heritage Dictionary*, third edition, the term refers to "a figure of speech in which an absent or imaginary person is represented as speaking."

Origen was well aware of prosopopeia as a rhetorical strategy and perceived Paul to have used it in Romans 7. Origen argued that Paul must be changing characters at certain points, because there was no other way to make sense of all Paul's claims. For example, when Paul says, "I was once alive apart from the law" (7:9), he cannot possibly be speaking for himself. Paul was born a Jew, "circumcised on the eighth day" (Philippians 3:5). Thus, there never was a time in which Paul could be described as having been alive apart from the law, especially if one assumes Paul here refers to the Mosaic law. Origen claimed that when Paul says, "I am of the flesh, sold into slavery under sin" in Romans 7:14, the ego— the "I"—cannot literally be Paul, because he most certainly does *not* consider himself a slave to sin. *That* is the condition of Gentiles apart from Christ. Paul clearly regards himself as capable of adequately resisting sin (Philippians 3:4-6). Origen thus argued that the ego with which Paul speaks in Romans 7:14-24 is a newly converted Gentile Christian believer, one who is still wrestling with the habits and desires of the old self. In other words, Paul uses the speech-in-character technique to speak in the persona of a Gentile, a Gentile confronting an evolving set of issues while progressing through the stages of moral and spiritual development necessary to reach the desired state of righteousness.

As Paul will go on to argue, while sin may hold sway with one's flesh, the self that is possessed of the Spirit is a "slave to the law of God" (7:25) and thus capable of resisting sin. In other words, in marked distinction to what would eventually become the prevailing Augustinian view of Romans, Origen saw the passage as an illustration of how the path to Christian salvation was also the path to moral transformation.

# PAUL AND THE LAW

Inextricably linked to the understanding of Paul as speaking of his own spiritual struggles is the view that Romans 7 is a powerful statement on the failure of both human morality and Judaism, in which morality constitutes a merit system leading to salvation. Traditional interpreters have understood the argument of Romans 7 to be essentially that the law is powerless to eradicate sin and thus powerless to lead one to God. In other words, in spite of the law being...well, *law*, it does not—and cannot—make a person righteous in God's sight. Yet ironically, righteousness is the prerequisite for salvation. On the one hand, there is no correlation between the ethical quality of a person's deeds and his or her salvation. On the other hand, God does not save wicked people; God only saves righteous people. In order to avoid confusion—or worse, apparent contradiction—Luther, Calvin, and other Reformers argued that "justification" actually means that God *imputes* righteousness to the faithful. *To impute* means "to charge" or "to credit." The idea is that God credits us this state of righteousness, even though no actual moral transformation has occurred.

Whatever Paul means to say in Romans 7, his understanding of law is key. Although he uses the word *law* in different ways, he most often uses it to refer to Law with a capital L, also known as the Torah or five books of Moses. Sometimes Paul just means God's teaching generally as contained in Scripture. And sometimes "law" is simply a synonym for Scripture. Chances are, if we have any experience of reading Paul's letters, we would think he regarded the law as a problem. Generally speaking, to most readers Paul sounds **more negative about law, say, in Galatians** than in Romans (a view reinforced by scholarship). But even when focusing on one letter, it is difficult for any reader to come away with a coherent understanding of Paul's view of the law.

However, if we take Paul's Jewish identity seriously, it is difficult to imagine how or why he would have had a problem with Jewish law. There is no necessary correlation between believing in Jesus and rejecting the Torah. The Prophets, the Psalms, and many non-canonical Jewish texts contemporary with Paul are full of eschatological expectations, and

> "For all who rely on the works of the law are under a curse; for it is written, 'Cursed is everyone who does not observe and obey all the things written in the book of the law.'"
> *(Galatians 3:10)*

often these expectations involve messianic figures—saviors sent by God to redeem the world. Yet there is no indication in any of these texts that a fervent belief in a messianic redeemer implies the end of the law. Paul quotes from texts like Leviticus and Deuteronomy as authoritative. Indeed, quotations, allusions, images, and characters from the Old Testament are so woven into the fabric of Romans, it is hard to imagine how Paul could have written anything in Romans without the Old Testament, which clearly serves as the theological bedrock of Paul's reflections on the righteousness of God in Romans.

So why in the world would Paul have a problem with Jewish law? Here the alternative tradition of interpretation can help us. For Origen and for many modern readers, Paul never does develop any notion of the law as a problem. On the contrary, it is "holy and just and good" (Romans 7:12). Rather, Paul's problem is with the Gentiles practicing Jewish law, whether they do it because they freely choose to or because other apostles or preacher-teachers are compelling them to become observant. It is not merely unnecessary or inappropriate; Paul regards it as unfaithful. God has already sent Christ to redeem the Gentiles *as Gentiles*. They do not need to become Jews in order to be children of God, because God has now fulfilled the promise made long ago: that Abraham would become the father of a multitude of nations.

If indeed Paul's audience is comprised of Gentiles, then he is perfectly consistent in his comments about Jewish law. And we can let go of the false assumption that there is something inherently wrong, inferior, or problematic about the law. We should instead remember that Paul is in fact speaking to a Gentile audience in his divinely ordained role as apostle to the Gentiles. Indeed, a careful reading of Romans 6:15-19 provides more clues to recognizing that Paul is speaking to Gentiles, especially when we think back to what he said about the idolatry and licentiousness of the Gentiles in Romans 1. Here in the midsection of Romans, Paul speaks as a pastor to the Gentiles in light of their history, their propensities (in his view, anyway), and their experience outside a covenanted, grace-filled life with God as he (a Jew!) imagines it. It seems Origen was right after all: Paul is imagining what it feels like to be a Gentile encountering the law for the first time and being indicted by the law for idolatry, the sin of sins!

But while Paul wants the Gentiles to acknowledge their sin, he makes clear it would be a mistake to start living as Jews. As he describes so beautifully later on in Romans 8, a new age is dawning: the messianic age. God is doing a new thing, as Isaiah once said (Isaiah 43:19). The "just requirement of the law" has been fulfilled by the offering of Christ (Romans 8:4). God has provided atonement for their past sins. To take on the mantle of full Jewish observance would be like saying no thanks to God. It would also be a terrible insult to the work of God's creation. The peace and harmony inspiring the visions of the messianic age would hardly mean much if all the world's people become one and the same; for God did not create humanity as one nation but as many. And God did not promise Abraham that he would be the father of one nation but a multitude of nations. Thus, God's children are not of a single kind, and salvation does not require that all people become one and the same. Gentiles demonstrate their faith in God not by becoming Jews but by trusting in God's promises, especially those concerning the salvation of Gentiles.

# INVITATION TO DISCIPLESHIP

Sin, law, and grace: They are all interwoven in this week's readings, just as they exist, interwoven together, as part of the fabric of our living. The conflict Paul addresses in Romans 7 is a conflict between following the desires of the flesh (into sin) and following the desires of the Spirit (into righteousness). His depiction of the law is in and of itself "holy and just and good" (7:12), reminding us of how often even our greatest efforts to follow the law—to keep the commandments, to do what we know is right—fail miserably. Our very humanness pushes us to fulfill our own selfish interests. And before we know it, sin is ruling our lives. We become slaves to it. We experience separation from God.

The law defines sin and how we should live our lives; but as Paul reminds us, following the law does not make us righteous before God. The righteousness of God is a gift to us, a gift of grace, and it comes through Christ, who, by fulfilling the law, rescues us "from this body of death" (7:24).

To live according to the Spirit and not gratify the desires of the flesh is Paul's charge to us, based on an amazing claim: "By sending his own Son in the likeness of sinful flesh, and to deal with sin, he [God] condemned sin in the flesh, so that the just requirement of the law might be fulfilled in us" (Romans 8:3-4). The assurance of grace for us is that even though our struggle with sin will not be over, we will be facing in the right direction.

# FOR REFLECTION

• In an Old Testament sense, the law defines boundaries and guide-lines for living. Identify the advantages and disadvantages of the law's relationship to faith. What made the law enticing to some Gentiles?

• How does sin become the master of someone's life? How do we gain freedom from sin?

• In Galatians 5:16-26, Paul speaks of life in the Spirit and life in the flesh. How would you describe the characteristics of each kind of life?

# Divine Purpose and Human Responsibility

*And in the very place where it was said to them,*
*"You are not my people," / there they shall be called*
*children of the living God.*

—Romans 9:26

## INTRODUCTION

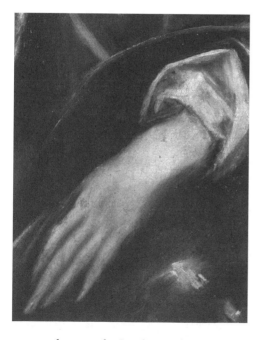

Up until the late twentieth century, commentators and theologians thought that whatever was important to know about Romans was contained in the first eight chapters. Given the dramatic way Chapter 8 ends, perhaps this is not surprising. However, the last two generations of scholars advocate a different orientation to the text, seeing Romans 9–11 as an integral part of Paul's larger argument. Many commentators even proclaim Romans 9–11 to be the climax of the letter. While it is a stretch to say there is consensus among scholars about what exactly constitutes the climax of Romans, it is possible to say this much: In these chapters, Paul explicitly addresses the relationship of Jews and Gentiles and the relationship of both to God as the time of salvation draws near. Most importantly, remember that the Jew-Gentile question is exactly where Paul started off his letter.

It is not difficult to see how Romans 9–11 returns to many of the themes and modes of rhetorical expression that marked Chapters 1–4. Paul cites Scripture frequently and speaks of the wrath and the righteousness of God. Less obvious is the relationship between Chapters 5–8 and 9–11, even though there are important links, especially between Chapters 8 and 9. For instance, Paul's apocalyptic view of the world is on display in Chapter 8 as he anxiously awaits the adoption and glorification of the children of God (8:19). Then, in Chapter 9, Paul turns to the question of Israel precisely because he knows from Scripture that adoption as children of God is a privilege possessed by Israel. The question on Paul's mind is, How then shall Israel's rejection of Christ be reconciled with God's promise of salvation? The answer does not come until Chapter 11. Yet in the meantime, we would do well to attend to the connections between Chapters 8–9 and, in particular, Paul's frequent invocations of the Old Testament.

# DAILY ASSIGNMENTS

The readings for this week concentrate on the complex nature of the divine-human relationship. As you read, look for any tension between the way that relationship is characterized in Romans 8 and Romans 9, as well as between Romans and the readings from the Old Testament.

## DAY ONE: Genesis 25:19-34; 27

These readings relate the story of Jacob's election over Esau, a story Paul invokes in Romans 9.

## DAY TWO: Romans 8:12-39

Paul articulates an inspiring, optimistic, and beautiful vision of the new creation being prepared for God's children. How does Paul's emphasis on the unfailing love of God here relate to the wrath of God that he forecast in Romans 1?

## DAY THREE: Romans 9:1-29

What does Paul mean when he says that God "has mercy on whomever he chooses, and he hardens the heart of whomever he chooses" (9:18)? What are the implications of this verse for understanding human free will?

## DAY FOUR: Job 1:1-11; 35; 40:1–42:6

How would you describe the lesson Job learns at the end of the Book of Job? Does it support the view of "God's purpose of election" as described by Paul in Romans 8–9?

## DAY FIVE: Commentary

Read the commentary in the participant book.

## DAY SIX: Romans 8:12–9:29

Reread the week's selection from Romans in light of the other assigned texts and the commentary.

# WHO ARE GOD'S CHILDREN?

In Romans 8, Paul describes how those "who are led by the Spirit of God" become "children of God" (8:14). If we read Romans 8 and 9 in relation to each other and also recall Paul's argument in Romans 4, we see that Paul regards the future inheritance of the children of God in the new age as the final realization of the inheritance God promised to Abraham and his descendants (8:14-17, 28-30; 9:6-9). We could say that the right to call Abraham "father" gives one the right to call God "Father" (4:16-18; 8:15-17; 9:4). To use Pauline terminology, the children of God are "called," "elected," or "chosen" according to God's will. Moreover, to be one of God's children is not merely a claim to status in name only. To be a child of God means salvation. Conversely, not being a child of God results in a different fate. The problem that arises—and takes up most of Paul's energy in Romans 9—is determining how the members of God's family are chosen and who is destined to enjoy eternal life as members of God's family in the age to come.

The spiritualized language of kinship and family used in relation to God in Romans 8 leads Paul in Romans 9 into a more concrete discussion of lineage rooted in biblical tradition. Israel, made up of the descendants of Abraham, is traditionally understood as God's chosen people. As is repeated in so many Old Testament texts, Israel belongs to God; Israel is God's portion (**Deuteronomy 32:9;** Leviticus 20:26). But as Paul says, "Not all Israelites truly belong to Israel, and not all of Abraham's children are his true descendants" (Romans 9:6-7).

> **"The LORD's own portion was his people, / Jacob his allotted share."**
> **(Deuteronomy 32:9)**

Paul's argument in Romans 9:6-18 is an elaboration of the one he made back in Chapter 4. Here, he makes an explicit point that being a physical descendant of Abraham is not a guarantee of God's favor. Like Isaac, Ishmael was a descendant of Abraham. In fact, Ishmael was Abraham's firstborn son. But God determined that Isaac would be blessed as Abraham's heir. Isaac is the child of promise, both in the sense that he fulfills the promise that God makes to Abraham, as Paul reminds us (Romans 9:9), and in the sense that he is the one who carries the promises to Abraham forward to the next generation. Like Isaac, Jacob is the second son, and he too is chosen by God to inherit the promises. Subsequently, Jacob's sons become the patriarchs of the twelve tribes of Israel, and quite simply, this is how Israel is constituted as God's people.

So while we could say that all Israelites are descendants of Abraham, not all of Abraham's descendants are Israelites. Notice how Paul again makes the point he made in Romans 4, namely that God's promise to Abraham that he would be the "father of many nations" means at least some Gentiles participate in Abraham's blessed lineage along with the Jews (9:24).

Yet in Romans 9, Paul is not simply restating his argument from Chapter 4 that Gentiles should also be counted among Abraham's descendants. Indeed, it is crucial that we recognize the challenges confronting us when we read Romans 9 honestly. According to the traditional interpretations of this chapter, what Paul is doing is appealing to the stories of Jacob and Esau and of Moses and Pharaoh to show that God "has mercy on whomever he chooses, and he hardens the heart of whomever he chooses" (9:18). So we are confronted by the idea that human action is irrelevant in determining who counts as God's elect. As unsettling as that sounds, it fits with a reading of Romans that emphasizes justification by faith apart from works. But when followed to their logical conclusion, Paul's comments in Romans 9 can lead to a deterministic view of the world that portrays God as capricious, eliminates human free will, and relegates morality to virtual irrelevance. And that may sound a bit disturbing.

# FREE WILL AND DETERMINISM

The history of Christian interpretation on Romans 9 reflects the centuries-long struggle to wrestle with the question of free will and determinism. The monotheism that characterizes Judaism, Christianity, and Islam proclaims faith in an omniscient and omnipotent God, a God who did not merely create the universe in a singular act but who also continually sustains and guides it, and whose divine purpose is embedded in the very fabric of creation. This is what we commonly call "divine providence."

In terms of the religious piety of Christians, the idea of divine providence can be quite comforting. Whether it is prayers of petition or words of comfort spoken to a person suffering, the implicit theological assumption is that God is actively working in the everyday lives of individuals. God is watching us; God is protecting us—no matter what, God is present, and God's purposes are playing out in our lives. Our goal is to discern whether we are following the path God has set before us. In Pauline terms, the Spirit works in the lives of believers to achieve God's purposes, and "all things work together for good for those who love God" (Romans 8:28).

But Paul's emphasis on God's foreknowledge and predestination in this section of Romans seemingly pushes beyond mere affirmations of divine providence. To be sure, the idea that God is in control of everything can easily become a theological and ethical conundrum. The more we emphasize the role of divine providence in the unfolding of events, the more we diminish the role of human responsibility. In its most robust form, divine providence imagines that God not only anticipates all events and their consequences but also predetermines them—*all* of them. This ultimately became the **position of Augustine**, a position later championed by Luther and Calvin, who exceeded even Augustine in the extent to which they maximized divine providence and minimized human agency. All of them grounded their views in Romans.

> **"Free will is most important. It exists, indeed, but of what value is it in those who are sold under sin?"[8]**
> *(Augustine)*

Paul's comments on God's choice of Jacob over Esau and on the hardening of Pharaoh's heart have prompted endless commentary, because they obviously call into question whether human beings really make their own choices. Augustine in particular was disturbed by the line of thought Paul pursues in Romans 9, especially in 9:16: "So it depends not on human will or exertion, but on God who shows mercy." Is the apostle really saying that human beings lack free will?

In truth, the overwhelming majority of commentators avoid construing Romans 9 as a full endorsement of divine determinism to the exclusion of free will, and for good reason. If everything that happens is in accordance with the will of God, where is there room for human responsibility? If human beings lack the freedom to make choices, how can they be held morally accountable? Paul himself anticipates this challenge when he asks, "Why then does he [God] still find fault? For who can resist his will?" (9:19).

The problem with a thoroughly deterministic view is that it calls into question the righteousness of God. The hardening of Pharaoh's heart could be interpreted to mean that God causes people to do bad things. The choice of Jacob over Esau, before they "had done anything good or bad" (9:11), implies that God does not reward the righteous and punish the wicked, as the words of the psalmists and the prophets proclaim. To put it bluntly, it would mean that God is capricious and arbitrary.

Augustine and Luther both dealt with these objections by admitting that humans in principle possess free will; in fact, God endowed humans with free will at the time of creation. But original sin caused the irreparable corruption of the will. Over time, human nature has become so habituated to sin that true freedom of choice has been lost. For all practical purposes, humans no longer have the ability to choose what is good. It is only God's mercy that allows some to avoid God's vengeance. Thus, when the Bible says that God hardened Pharaoh's heart, it should not be taken to mean that God bears responsibility for Pharaoh's display of wicked defiance. The fault lies with Pharaoh. The hardening of his heart means simply that God chose not to have mercy on him. One must assume it served God's purpose not to have mercy on him while also admitting that God's purposes are indecipherable.

Virtually every interpreter of Romans begins with the same basic theological assumptions that informed Augustine and Luther: God is an all-knowing, all-powerful God who is righteous in every way. What distinguishes Augustine and Luther and the majority of interpreters since the Reformation is that they were especially keen to uphold a vision of God as *completely* all-knowing, all-powerful, and all-good. Conversely, humans lack knowledge and understanding of God, lack the power to affect God's purposes, and—last but not least—lack the ability to do what is right. The assumption seems to be that any attribution of knowledge, purposeful action, or moral virtue to human nature seems to detract from the glory of God, as if the qualities that characterize divinity and those that characterize humanity were inversely proportionate.

> Virtually every interpreter of Romans begins with the same basic theological assumptions that informed Augustine and Luther: God is an all-knowing, all-powerful God who is righteous in every way.

This same perspective informs the traditional interpretation of Romans as a treatise on justification by faith. That is, God credits righteousness to human beings so they may be saved. Whether individually or collectively, human beings do not possess righteousness, and there is nothing they can do to get it. Therefore, salvation would be utterly unattainable except for the mercy of God. Recall what Paul says by quoting Isaiah in Romans 9:28: "For the Lord will execute his sentence on the earth quickly and decisively." Given the extent to which Paul speaks of the need for human righteousness in the face of God's eschatological judgment, when all humankind is held accountable before God, Paul hardly reflects the view that human beings bear no responsibility for their behavior. In fact, too much focus on what Paul says here about the absolute omniscience, omnipotence, and perfection of God—at the expense of human freedom and agency—ignores much of what he says elsewhere in Romans.

> Origen believed free will was integral to the redemption of the world. He viewed humans as actively participating in their own salvation by desiring to know God and by cooperating with God in doing God's will.

However, prior to Augustine, there was an old and venerable tradition of reading Romans 8–9 as describing a divine-human partnership in bringing about redemption. In marked distinction to the Augustinian-Lutheran line of thought, Origen believed free will was integral to the redemption of the world. He viewed humans as actively participating in their own salvation by desiring to know God and by cooperating with God in doing God's will. Cooperation with God means that humans must pursue what is good and shun what is evil. God takes the initiative in calling people, but human agency plays its part in working toward salvation. Those who are called choose either to respond in faithful obedience or to resist, but the choice is theirs to make.

Origen addressed Paul's language of foreknowledge and predestination in Romans 8–9 by interpreting the language more subtly. Indeed, Origen (echoing many modern scholars) said that Paul used words like *calling, foreknowledge, predestination, election,* and *justification* in discrete ways—that is, distinct in meaning. By contrast, interpreters like Augustine and Luther treated those terms as having similar meanings. So what's the difference?

Romans 8:28-30 provides an excellent illustration of the difference. In these verses, Paul provides a kind of summary of the process that results in salvation. In making his summary, Paul connects God's foreknowledge to predestination, predestination to being called, and being called to being justified and, finally, to being glorified. Luther interpreted all these terms as synonyms for salvation, because he understood God's foreknowledge to bear inevitable results. In other words, there is absolutely nothing that can interfere with God's will. God's foreknowledge of something is as good as the reality of it. Thus, to be "called" is to be "justified" is to be "glorified"—it all adds up to the same result: salvation. (And not being called leads inevitably to the opposite result.) Thus, according to the traditional interpretation of Romans, which sees Paul as an advocate for divine determinism, it is inconceivable to imagine any variable, including human free will, as affecting the outcome of something God desires. Everything that happens has been predetermined.

By contrast, Origen interpreted Romans 8:28-30 as stages in a process of transformation (much like he interpreted Romans 7:7-25). And the first stage of the process is that God calls everyone to salvation. What happens in subsequent stages depends on whether or not the person responds appropriately to God's call. According to Origen, the language of foreknowledge and predestination that follows in 8:29-30 applies *only* to those who have responded to God's call. God does not predestine, elect, or justify anyone who has not already chosen to cooperate with God in God's purposes. Thus, not everything that happens in the universe is the simple realization of God's will. God's will for creation can only be fully realized when created beings cooperate with God to bring about God's good purposes. If we follow Origen's reading of Romans, we are not compelled to see Romans as an endorsement of divine determinism. The concept of divine providence is more limited in this case, but the possibilities of divine-human cooperation are much more hopeful than they are with the traditional view, and the scope of salvation is potentially much larger.

# INVITATION TO DISCIPLESHIP

Thinking the end of time was near, Paul looks at how members of God's family are chosen and who is destined to enjoy eternal life in the age to come. God initiates the relationship between God and humankind. Some interpret this relationship as being predetermined, with humans lacking any real choice or free will. However, as with any relationship, in order for the relationship to be genuine and for love to abound, both partners must be active participants.

God is still active in the world today and desires to be in relationship with us. Conversely, we seek out God's presence and activity in the events of our lives and desire to be in relationship with God. Generally speaking, we all likely operate out of some notion of divine providence and human responsibility. Some of us may emphasize God's role in the world; others of us may emphasize the role of human agency in the unfolding of events. Regarding our relationship with God, though, ultimately we do have a choice: Either we respond to God in faithful obedience, or we resist God's invitation and go our own way. To choose to become active participants in the divine-human relationship is to desire to know God and to cooperate with God in doing God's will.

# FOR REFLECTION

• How would you define God's divine purpose? How is that purpose carried out in the world today?

• How would you describe your partnership with God? What role do you think human beings play in the unfolding events of our world?

• Recall this statement from the commentary: "God's will for creation can only be fully realized when created beings cooperate with God to bring about God's good purposes" (page 77). What does this statement mean to you?

# The Salvation of Israel and the Nations

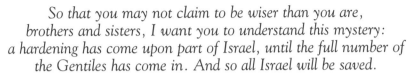

*So that you may not claim to be wiser than you are,*
*brothers and sisters, I want you to understand this mystery:*
*a hardening has come upon part of Israel, until the full number of*
*the Gentiles has come in. And so all Israel will be saved.*

—Romans 11:25-26

## INTRODUCTION

Thanks to a post-Holocaust perspective among Christian interpreters and theologians, Romans 9–11 has received more attention in the past fifty years than at any time in history. The centuries-long assumption that the Jews had been rejected by God because they did not believe in Christ and were replaced by the Gentiles who had faith in Christ was thought to be grounded in Romans. Reconsideration of this belief and those passages that seemingly support it was long overdue. So let's take a fresh look at Romans 9–11; for there, Paul explicitly reflects on the tension between God's unique relationship with the people of Israel (well attested to in Scripture, of course) and God's relationship with all of humanity.

In studying this portion of Romans, we should acknowledge that Paul's understanding of God is primarily informed by the vision of God revealed in the oracles of Isaiah. There, God is proclaimed as the one and only Creator and Sustainer of the entire world. In other words, the God Israel knows as the God of Abraham, Isaac, and Jacob is also the God of all humanity. Yet God chose Israel from among the nations to be God's very own people, and thus God's relationship to Israel is unique among the nations. As Paul emphasizes several times in Romans, Israel has enjoyed God's favor and received promises of salvation. The crucial question for Paul in Romans 9–11 is, What is Israel's role now that Christ has come, now that a new age is dawning, an age in which Gentiles will also become part of God's family? What complicates Paul's answer is that the vast majority of Israel did not realize who Christ was or what he signified.

# DAILY ASSIGNMENTS

As you read through the texts this week, bear in mind the following question: If God is God of the whole world, why would God distinguish Israel from other nations? What is the purpose of God having a specially chosen people? How do we reconcile the particular God we know from Scripture—the God who interacted with particular people and places at particular times—with the God we envision as the Creator of all humanity and Sustainer of the entire universe?

## DAY ONE: Isaiah 2:2-4; Zechariah 8

These texts represent a tradition found in some prophetic texts known as the "ingathering of the nations." Some scholars believe Paul was inspired to pursue his mission to the Gentiles by this tradition.

## DAY TWO: Romans 9:30–10:21

When Paul says (quoting from the prophet Joel), "Everyone who calls on the name of the Lord shall be saved" (10:13), to whom does the word *Lord* refer?

## DAY THREE: Romans 11

Note the complex way Paul sees Israel and the nations participating in the process of salvation.

## DAY FOUR: Jeremiah 31:31-37; Isaiah 59:9-21; Micah 7:14-20

Paul's emphasis on the irrevocable nature of God's promises to Israel is rooted in longstanding biblical tradition.

## DAY FIVE: Commentary

Read the commentary in the participant book.

## DAY SIX: Romans 9:30–11:36

Reread the week's selection from Romans in light of the other assigned texts and the commentary.

# CHRIST AND THE LAW

Like the opening verses of Chapter 9, Paul begins Romans 10 by expressing anguish about the fate of Israel. But Paul's concern slips quickly into the background, and the apostle resumes the critique of Israel he began in 9:30-33. At first glance, his comments in Romans 9:30–10:4 depict Israel as a people who observe the law in the hope of attaining righteousness and thus salvation. According to Paul's critique, by so doing, the people of Israel arrogantly rely on their own works rather than on faith, which comes from God. Their arrogance leads to ignorance of God's will. Hence, Israel rejects Christ when she should have rejected the law. As Paul says in Romans 10:4, "Christ is the end of the law."

But what does Paul mean by that? Is he unambiguously claiming that Christ supersedes the law? Perhaps not. The word *end* translates **the Greek word *telos*** in Romans 10:4, a word with many possible connotations. The very choice of the English word *end* for *telos* already forces a certain interpretation upon the verse. As a result, Romans 10:4 typically is read to mean that the coming of Christ has *literally* put an end to the law. Put another way, the law is no longer necessary as a mediator between humans and God, because Christ functions as a superior mediator.

> **According to one Greek-English lexicon, the Greek word *telos* (*τέλος*) means "end," in the sense of: (a) termination or cessation; (b) the last part or conclusion; or (c) the end or goal toward which a movement is being directed.[9]**

According to the tradition of interpretation established by Augustine and Luther, the primary purpose of the law had been to bring people to the realization that they are sinners, helpless to reform themselves by their own efforts and thus without hope of "achieving" redemption. In other words, the law does not lead to salvation; rather, it leads to the realization that human beings can do nothing to effect salvation. At best, the law leads to the realization that Christ is necessary for salvation. Therefore, Christ supersedes the law, both in historical terms as applied to the history of the human race and in terms of the religious development of each human being.

Another way to understand what Paul means in Romans 10:4 is to accept another but no less appropriate translation of the Greek word *telos*. Besides meaning "end," the word can also convey the sense of a goal, purpose, or fulfillment. Thus, Romans 10:4 could just as well read, "Christ is the goal of the law." In light of this reading, the advent of Christ does not imply the termination of the law but rather the fulfillment of it. The law foretold Christ's coming and the eschatological culmination of history that Christ initiates. Another way to make the same point is to say that God's ultimate purpose is fulfilled through Christ. The purpose of God's law was to instruct people in God's will. As the expression of God's will, the Torah included instructions about how to worship God and how to lead a righteous life, but it also included prophetic forecasts of the future so that all humanity ultimately might have insight into God's ultimate plan for creation.

Though the law was given by Moses to Israel, all people are ultimately accountable to it. But not everyone is accountable to it in the same way. There are laws that pertain only to priests, others that pertain only to men, and others that pertain only to women. Similarly, there are laws that apply exclusively to Israelites. But the Torah also communicates God's expectations of humanity in general. The most important thing God desires from human beings is the recognition that God is the one and only God, a God of righteousness and compassion, who created the world and who determines its ultimate destiny. In other words, God's will is the redemption of the world. Paul therefore proclaims, "Christ is the end of the law so that there may be righteousness for everyone who believes," because Christ has achieved exactly that.

# ISRAEL'S ROLE IN REDEMPTION

If indeed Paul does not think Christ "trumps" the Torah, how do we explain the many critical comments he makes about Israel in Romans 9–11? If Paul is not condemning Jews for their reliance on works of the law and the consequent lack of faith in Christ in which such reliance results, why does he describe Israel as ignorant and unenlightened (10:2-3, 19)? Why would Paul say that "Israel failed to obtain what it was seeking. The elect obtained it, but the rest were hardened" (11:7)? Why imply that God has abandoned Israel, or at least those members of Israel who do not believe in Christ (11:20)?

There is no doubt that Paul takes Israel to task in these chapters of Romans. The difference between traditional ways of reading them and other perspectives lies with our understanding *what* Paul's complaint against Israel is and determining *who* Israel is. Let's take up the "what" question first and the "who" question later. In the meantime, we will assume "Israel" simply refers to the same people the Old Testament speaks of and that Jews understand as a God-given name for their collective identity as God's people.

Paul's critical comments about Israel's lack of faith in Romans 10–11 should not be taken to mean that the people of Israel have been faithless and disobedient in general, as later Christian tradition assumed. On the contrary, Paul's accusations of Israel's ignorance and unbelief refer to something specific: Israel does not recognize Christ as the firstborn of the new age, the one who has been charged by God to oversee the transition from the old age to the new one, the age in which all the nations are reconciled to God and to each other. Paul emphasizes the singularity of Christ's lordship on earth because it represents the oneness of God as well as the harmonious integration of all peoples when they unite in worshiping the one God (Romans 10:11-13). The confession to which Paul refers in Romans 10:9—"Jesus is Lord"—was probably intended primarily for Gentiles who had served various other gods and lords (1 Corinthians 8:5-6). The fact that Israel does not recognize the lordship of Christ indicates she does not recognize God's purposes at work in Christ, and for Paul, this constitutes Israel's lack of faith.

If Israel had the faith Paul wants them to have, Israel as a whole would follow in Paul's footsteps and take up the task of preaching to the Gentiles. Paul probably did not envision every Jew becoming a missionary. But he likely expected that the current leadership of Israel would at least sponsor his missionary work as well as that of the other apostles.

> "You are my witnesses, says the LORD, / and my servant whom I have chosen, / so that you may know and believe me / and understand that I am he. / Before me no god was formed, / nor shall there be any after me."
> (Isaiah 43:10)

In the words of Isaiah, God charged Israel to be a "light to the nations" (49:6). God chose the people of Israel so that they would serve as a witness to the world that the God of Israel is the one and only God, Creator and Redeemer, besides whom there is no other (**Isaiah 43:10**; 49:6-7; see also 56:1-8). Thus, Paul's critique of Israel is not that Israel's observance of the Torah has prevented her from having faith in Christ. On the contrary, the problem is that Israel is not heeding the words of the Torah carefully enough. God declared "the end from the beginning" (Isaiah

84

46:10). It is time for the ingathering of the nations. It is the time when all the Gentiles shall forsake their lifeless gods and recognize the God of Israel, the one true living God. The death and resurrection of Jesus signaled that God had initiated this process of cosmic salvation. Unfortunately, Israel did not perceive that the time for salvation had come. Unlike the Gentile believers in Rome to whom Paul writes his letter, Israel did not realize what time it was (Romans 13:11).

Israel's rejection of Christ surely constitutes a failure on Israel's part, but it is not a complete failure. Paul interprets Israel's failure to embrace Christ as part of God's plan for achieving the ingathering of the nations. Just as God once hardened Pharaoh's heart in order to proclaim God's name throughout the earth (Romans 9:17), now it seems God hardens Israel's heart for a similar purpose: to bring salvation to the Gentiles (Romans 11:11, 25). Israel's rejection has protracted God's timetable for salvation, thus giving more time for the nations to hear and respond to God's call. Israel's rejection of Christ means greater mercy for the Gentiles.

Because God's promises to Israel are irrevocable, Paul assumes Israel's rejection must be temporary. God will not save the Gentiles apart from Israel, because God promised that all nations would be blessed through the lineage of Abraham (Genesis 12:3). Israel is the agent through which God works the redemption of the world. God's salvation of the Gentiles occurs in conjunction with the salvation of Israel, because redemption depends on the nations forsaking their idols and joining Israel in worship and praise of the one and only God. Thus, the scenario Paul describes in Romans 11 views Israel and the Gentile nations as mutually interdependent. Each needs the other in order for the world to be reconciled to God.

# "ALL ISRAEL WILL BE SAVED"

One of the great puzzlements of Romans 9–11 is the relationship between Paul's statement in 9:6 that "not all Israelites truly belong to Israel" and his subsequent claim in 11:26 that "all Israel will be saved." To reconcile these two seemingly contradictory statements, many commentators claim that part of Paul's argument in Romans 9–11 is intended to redefine who Israel is. Whom exactly is Paul talking about in these chapters? Christian tradition eventually concluded that the church was the true Israel of which Paul spoke; all those who believe in Christ now constitute Israel. The old Israel was rejected by God, just as they rejected Christ. And yet, Paul is emphatic in 11:26: He doesn't say, "The faithful of Israel will be saved," or "A remnant of

Israel will be saved"; he says, "*All* Israel will be saved." Why would Paul say "all" when he has earlier emphasized rather strongly that "not all Israelites truly belong to Israel"?

Recall the verses where Paul explicitly refers to Israel. In most instances, the context indicates that Paul uses the term to refer to the Jewish people as a whole. He comes pretty close to providing a definition the first time he uses the term, when he describes Israel's privileges (adoption, the covenants, giving of the law, and others in 9:4-5). Paul uses the term essentially the same way any other Jew of his day would use it, which is consistent with the way it is used in the Old Testament—namely, to refer collectively to the descendants of Abraham, whom God chose to be God's people.

Of course, up until Romans 11, most of what Paul says about Israel is negative. He uses citations from all over Scripture to demonstrate Israel's failure to fulfill God's expectations. Therefore, clearly in Romans 9–10, Paul is referring to the same people of Israel spoken of in the Old Testament. What trouble we have connecting the Israel discussed in Romans and the Israel of biblical tradition is likely rooted in our inability to conceive that Paul would affirm the salvation of *all* Israel.

But let's consider the idea that Paul meant what he said: All Israel will indeed be saved. Two assumptions prevent us from taking Paul at his word. The first is rooted in a misunderstanding of the term *remnant* (9:27; 11:5). Modern readers typically understand the remnant as referring to a select group of fortunate individuals left standing at the end. When Paul says, "Only a remnant…will be saved," in the context of discussing Israel (9:27), readers assume he means only a tiny fraction of Israelites will be saved—presumably those like Paul who believe in Jesus. Given this assumption, it is not surprising that we are confused when Paul subsequently says, "All Israel will be saved." Which is it: a *remnant* of Israel or *all* of Israel who will be saved?

However, the remnant is not the equivalent of those who are chosen by God to be God's children forever. The remnant serves a temporary function: the reunification of God with God's people. The idea is there will always be a remnant of Israel left in order to insure that Israel can be reconstituted and revitalized as God's people, even when a majority of Israel has gone astray, been disobedient, or been destroyed. The remnant represents the thread of continuity from one generation to the next or, in this case, from one eon to the next. Thus, the remnant is the guarantee that God's promises to Israel are never in danger of failing. That is why Paul says the remnant is "chosen by grace" (11:5). So even if 99.9 percent have stumbled, the remnant insures

God can maintain God's fidelity; "for the gifts and calling of God are irrevocable" (11:29).

A second misleading assumption is to read the word *all* in "all Israel will be saved" as meaning that each and every individual will be saved. In other words, we tend to conceptualize salvation only in terms of individuals. By contrast, Paul conceives of salvation in communal terms. That is to say, Paul imagines the salvation of whole peoples or communities. Therefore, when Paul says, "All Israel will be saved," he does not mean each and every Israelite. He means Israel as a whole will be saved. Israel will survive the transition from the old age to the new one and will be collectively reconstituted as the children of God. The same principle applies to the phrase "the full number of the Gentiles" (Romans 11:25). Paul does not mean each and every Gentile will be saved. He means all the Gentiles as nations; he means all the world's various nations will participate in God's final redemption. Paul sees salvation not as a matter to be worked out between each individual and God; he sees it as communal and cosmic. Salvation is a synonym for the redemption of the world.

> Paul sees salvation not as a matter to be worked out between each individual and God; he sees it as communal and cosmic. Salvation is a synonym for the redemption of the world.

As we progress through Romans 9–11, we see how Paul places greater and greater emphasis on inclusiveness. Expressions such as "full inclusion" and "full number" and the repetitions of "all" and "everyone" indicate that Paul does in fact envision universal redemption. However, the communal and cosmic nature of redemption means that we need not imagine the inclusion of every single individual who ever lived. Perhaps there are some wicked individuals who are irredeemable and therefore cannot participate in the new creation. Paul mentions the possibility that some people will be "cut off" (11:22). However, even Origen believed that while some individuals might have to suffer punishment temporarily in order to be transformed, eventually every single soul who ever lived would be redeemed. Nevertheless, a universal vision of redemption *does* mean that the variety of peoples who inhabit the earth are included in the family of God of the new creation. Most importantly, they are included in their variety. They do not become the same people. Rather, all the peoples are adopted as children of God. Since everyone will recognize God as their Father, all will understand themselves as kin;

there will no longer be strangers and foreigners. But Gentile need not become Jew, nor Jew Gentile. God created a multiplicity of nations, and a multiplicity of nations God will redeem.

# INVITATION TO DISCIPLESHIP

Throughout Romans, Paul's focus is on God and the extension of God's family to include not only Israel but all of humanity. As stated in the introduction of this session, the crucial question for Paul in Romans 9–11 is, What is Israel's role now that Christ has come and now that Gentiles are a part of God's family? A similarly crucial question for us is, What is our role now that Christ has come and we are a part of God's family?

At least part of our role is to be agents of God's redemption or salvation, a redemption that reaches out to all and desires for all to be saved. If indeed Paul sees salvation not as a matter simply to be worked out between each individual and God but rather a reality with both communal and cosmic dimensions, then we need to enlarge our vision of God's redemption. We need to focus more on beating our swords into plowshares and our spears into pruning hooks, and learning war no more; for Paul's broad vision of redemption means not only that "all Israel will be saved" (11:26) and be a part of the family of God's new creation, but so will the variety of peoples who inhabit this earth with us. So in our role as agents of God's redemption, we are called to think not only of our own individual salvation but also the salvation and redemption of the nations.

# FOR REFLECTION

- What is your understanding of God's unique relationship to the people of Israel? How did the week's readings and the session commentary inform your understanding?

- How does the image of salvation as the redemption of whole peoples or communities support or challenge your idea of God's purpose for the world? What is the basis for your understanding of salvation?

- As God's agent of salvation in the world, how do you see yourself helping God carry out this task?

# Love and Humility Are the Making of God's Kingdom

*For by the grace given to me I say to everyone among you
not to think of yourself more highly than you ought to think,
but to think with sober judgment, each according to
the measure of faith that God has assigned.*

—Romans 12:3

## INTRODUCTION

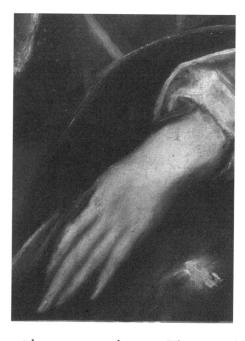

It is characteristic of Paul to put ethical exhortations at the end of his letters. And that is exactly what we find in Paul's Letter to the Romans. Much of what he says in the final chapters sounds similar to teachings found in his other letters, particularly in First Corinthians. Some of what Paul says even seems to reflect Jesus' teachings in the Sermon on the Mount. However, the tendency among scholars has been to neglect Romans 12–15 and Paul's ethical teachings in general. This may be partially the result of their interpreting Paul's primary concern to be distinguishing between "works" (or ethics) and "faith" (or theology)—that is, relegating works to an inferior position with respect to salvation. There can be no doubt that Paul focuses his energy on what people should do in these final chapters. So of course, then, any reader of Romans who understands its main message as justification by faith would find little of interest in these chapters.

Nevertheless, these last chapters demand our attention, if for no other reason than because Paul returns to his theology of mission, explicitly addressing the Jew-Gentile question one final time. Before outlining his travel plans (Romans 15:22-29) and sending along his greetings (16:1-23), Paul reminds the Romans of what has been accomplished in Christ both for Jews and for Gentiles. "For I tell you that Christ has become a servant of the circumcised on behalf of the truth of God in order that he might confirm the promises given to the patriarchs, and in order that the Gentiles might glorify God for his mercy" (15:8-9a). However, this passage concludes with a string of quotations about what the good news means specifically for the Gentiles (15:9b-13). This should be no surprise. After all, Paul is the apostle to the *Gentiles*, and his stated purpose is to "bring about the obedience of faith among all the Gentiles" (1:5; see also 15:18).

# DAILY ASSIGNMENTS

As you read through the concluding selection of texts, keep the following questions in mind: How do Paul's ethical teachings compare to those we find in the Old Testament? Does Paul diminish the importance of works in favor of faith, as Augustine and Luther claimed? Or does Paul envision a kind of faith that includes doing certain kinds of works?

## DAY ONE: Exodus 20:1-17; Deuteronomy 30

These readings illustrate how acting in accordance with the law was not so much about achieving moral perfection but rather about being faithful to God and the covenant God had established with Israel.

## DAY TWO: Romans 12–13

In what ways does Paul's ethical instruction resemble the ethical teachings found in other parts of the Bible?

## DAY THREE: Romans 14:1–15:13

What kinds of people do you think Paul is referring to when he speaks of the "weak" and the "strong"?

## DAY FOUR: Isaiah 55:1–56:8; 1 Corinthians 10; 12:12–13:13

In Isaiah's vision of salvation, humanity is no longer alienated from God, and all peoples live in peace and harmony. How do you think this influenced Paul's vision of salvation?

## DAY FIVE: Commentary

Read the commentary in the participant book.

## DAY SIX: Romans 12–15:13

Reread the week's selection from Romans in light of the other assigned texts and the commentary.

# SPIRITUAL WORK

Romans 12 opens with Paul exhorting his audience to be "holy and accept-able to God, which is your spiritual worship." The word here translated as "spiritual" could also be translated as "thoughtful" or "conscientious." However, the word translated as "worship" would be better rendered as "serv-ice" (from the Greek word *latreia*). In a secular context, latreia refers to ordi-nary work performed by a slave or a laborer. When used in a religious context, it usually refers to the work of priests in performing sacrifices or other rituals and is sometimes translated as "worship." Paul used the verbal form of the same word earlier in describing his missionary work (1:9). Insofar as Romans 12:1-2 functions as an introduction to the ethical instruction that will follow, Paul signals to his audience that he is about to instruct them in how they can prop-erly render service to God as well as to fellow human beings.

Paul believes those who have received the good news should act in such a way that anticipates the ethos of the new creation he described earlier in Romans 8. As a result, the ethical instructions in Romans 12 describe the kinds of social relations that characterize the new age: Paul stresses that believ-ers must love one another selflessly, in utter humility, so that they live in per-fect harmony and in peace with everyone. This is what life looks like in the kingdom of God.

Remember that while the traditional interpretation of Romans excludes works from playing any role whatsoever in salvation, the other interpretation to which we have appealed in this study views righteous works as an essential part of the process that leads to salvation. The right sort of conduct is a response of the faith that leads to salvation. In other words, salvation depends on human will as well as divine will. God's purposes are ultimately fulfilled when those whom God has chosen reciprocate by choosing to do God's work. Thus, Paul's exhortations to "hate what is evil, hold fast to what is good; love one another..., be patient in suffering," and "live peaceably with all" (12:9-10, 12, 18) reflect the spiri-tual work that brings about the kingdom of God. The conduct to which Paul exhorts the com-munity of believers constitutes the sort of cooperation with God that Abraham exhibited in conceiving Isaac. Indeed, it is the same kind

> God's purposes are ultimately fulfilled when those whom God has chosen reciprocate by choosing to do God's work.

of divine-human cooperation that Origen imagined—the kind that participates with God in working toward salvation.

So When Paul says, "Salvation is nearer to us now than when we became believers" (Romans 13:11), he does not mean he has some special insight into God's schedule for salvation. (Elsewhere Paul warns against such speculations: 1 Thessalonians 5:2). Rather, he encourages his audience to remain steadfast in anticipating redemption—and that means maintaining conduct befitting life in the new age, conduct best summed up by the call to love one another (Romans 13:8-10). Paul's message in 13:11-14 resembles that spoken by many Old Testament prophets, especially the oracles of Isaiah: "Thus says LORD: / Maintain justice, and do what is right, / for soon my salvation will come, / and my deliverance be revealed. / Happy is the mortal who does this" (Isaiah 56:1-2). Thus, as he clearly states in these closing chapters, for Paul, good works *do* matter to salvation.

# THE KEY INGREDIENT IN PAUL'S ETHIC OF LOVE: HUMILITY

As the title of this lesson suggests, the two virtues Paul stresses most strongly in his concluding remarks to the Romans are love and humility. Paul's emphasis on love is not hard to spot, since he uses the word *love* (*agape* in Greek) frequently in Romans 12–13. Furthermore, even those who do not know much about Paul are familiar with his famous poem about love in 1 Corinthians 13. Between 1 Corinthians 13 and Romans 8, this apostle to the Gentiles bequeathed to the Western world some of the most powerful descriptions of love ever penned.

Unfortunately, ancient Greek had nearly a half-dozen words for our English word *love*. The kind of love of which Paul speaks both in First Corinthians and Romans is the self-giving kind. So self-giving is Paul's kind of love that humility is essential to the authentic expression of it. One can clearly see this when he defines love in First Corinthians: "Love is patient, love is kind; love is not envious or boastful or arrogant or rude.... It bears all things, believes all things, hopes all things, endures all things" (13:4-7). Although Paul writes poetically here, he articulates a most fundamental ethical principle. In Pauline terms, the goal of love is to treat others so that we always build them up, even if those same others have acted in such a way as to tear us down (Romans 14:19; **15:2-3a;** 1 Corinthians 10:23-24). It is no coincidence that Paul's reflections on love follow his description of communal harmony using the metaphor of the body in both Romans (12:4-10; 13:8-10) and First Corinthians (12:12–13:13).

> "Each of us must please our neighbor for the good purpose of building up the neighbor. For Christ did not please himself."
> *(Romans 15:2-3a)*

Humility is not just a mental disposition; it is an attitude that should result in life lived in accordance with the love ethic. One of the first specific ethical directives Paul articulates in Romans is a warning "not to think of yourself more highly than you ought to think" (12:3). Indeed, most of Paul's ethical imperatives in Romans 12 involve what we might deem deliberate acts of humility. We should not to be haughty or pretend to be wiser than we really are. We should give more honor to others than we receive, and we should never avenge the wrongs we have suffered. It is easy to see how Paul can sum up his entire ethic by saying, "The one who loves another has fulfilled the law," and "Love is the fulfilling of the law" (13:8, 10). The similarity between what Paul says about love in Romans and what he says in his other epistles demonstrates that agape was a vital ethical principle that informed Paul's life and thought. (In addition to First Corinthians, see Galatians 5:13-26; 1 Thessalonians 3:11-13; 4:9-12.)

# SUBJECT TO AUTHORITIES

Keeping in mind the priority Paul gives to humility in these final chapters, consider one particularly troublesome passage: Romans 13:1-7. Many interpreters and students of Paul's letters simply cannot imagine Paul condoning complete submission to political authority irrespective of the moral quality of that authority. For those of us on this side of the twentieth century, we readily imagine Hitler's Third Reich, the apartheid regime in South Africa, or the Khmer Rouge in Southeast Asia and think, *Shouldn't we resist such authority rather than willingly subject ourselves to such evil?* Surely Paul, of all people, living under the corrupt and cruel Roman emperor Nero would not really call for submission to that kind of authority. With that in mind, some modern commentators have argued that Romans 13:1-7 is not authentic to Paul.

However, most commentators think Paul was not making a universal declaration advocating submission to all forms of political authority. For example,

**Christians who were martyred by Roman authorities** resisted the will of those authorities by their refusal to make sacrifices to the emperor, who was considered a god. Given Paul's vehement opposition to idolatry, surely he would have commended such Christians for not renouncing their faith. Put simply, some forms of political resistance met with Paul's approval. After all, we know from Paul's Letter to the Philippians that he himself was imprisoned by Roman authorities (1:7, 13-14). He must therefore have offended them in some way or another.

> "The martyrs in Christ disarm the principalities and powers with Him, and they share His triumph as fellows of His sufferings, becoming in this way also fellows of the courageous deeds wrought in His sufferings."[10]
> (Origen)

Thus, it seems highly unlikely that Paul meant to rule out the possibility of political resistance altogether. More likely, he is simply exhorting the audience to apply to the political and civic realms the same ethic of humility that operates within the community of believers. Even though believers now confess Jesus as Lord, Paul still expects them to treat all others with respect, including government officials "to whom honor is due" (13:7); for all anyone knows, those officials may be unwitting agents in God's plan of salvation.

# THE WEAK AND THE STRONG

When we come to Paul's discussion regarding the weak and the strong in Romans 14, we wade into another area where Pauline scholars have spilled a lot of ink. Exactly who are the weak and the strong? The reigning theory is that the weak are Jewish Christians who continue to observe Jewish dietary laws and certain rituals associated with the sabbath and other festival days. The strong are assumed to be Gentile Christians who place no value on these practices and believe they reflect some sort of spiritual weakness. Moreover, according to the dominant view, the weak are called "weak" precisely because of their adherence to Jewish observances. However, this reconstruction of the historical situation is highly speculative; for Paul never explicitly connects the weak to ethnic Jews or Jewish Christians. He also does not say that the weakness of the group labeled "weak" lies in their maintaining a commitment to traditional Jewish observances.

On the contrary, it would not make any sense for Paul to judge the weak for their opinions about such matters, because the entire thrust of Paul's message in Romans 14 is a warning against judging others for holding certain opinions on relatively minor matters. Ironically, virtually all commentators recognize this to be Paul's main message in this chapter. On one hand, they consider Paul's teaching in Romans 14 as connected to Chapters 12–13: We should conduct ourselves with humility, which first of all means we should avoid judging others as good or bad, right or wrong, and leave the judging to God. On the other hand, virtually all the same commentators then proceed to disparage the views of the weak, explaining that their faith is weak because it depends on certain observances and, furthermore, that the weak are the cause of dissension in the Roman church.

But wait—remember that Paul's love ethic stresses the preeminence of humility; in fact, that has been Paul's focus since Romans 12. Chapter 14 continues the same emphasis on humility, only here appealing specifically to the relations between the weak and the strong. Although Paul begins the chapter by exhorting each group to refrain from condemning the other, it quickly becomes clear that his target audience is not the weak and their desire to eat only vegetables but rather the strong who believe in "eating anything" (14:2). In other words, Paul does not admonish the weak for their practices. He does not attempt to correct their opinion as if it were a misunderstanding that compromised their faith or, worse, threatened their salvation. Quite the contrary, *Paul admonishes the strong* for their judgmental attitude (14:10) and for failing to consider that their behavior has the potential to cause their fellow brother or sister to fall (14:15, 20). Perhaps most remarkable is that Paul admonishes the strong for *their* eating habits, which are a hindrance and a stumbling block to others (14:13, 21). In summary, Paul condemns the strong for their judgmental attitude toward the weak and for their behavior, but he never condemns the weak for their beliefs *or* their practices.

In light of these observations, it is most likely that the weak are labeled "weak" not because of any particular beliefs or practices but rather because they have less power and influence than the strong. The strong are attempting to coerce the weak, who are the underdogs in this dispute. According to Paul, the strong deserve rebuke because they are not conducting themselves in accord with the love ethic required for participation in God's work of redemption. They lack humility. They are convinced they are right in their views and can therefore impose their will on others. By contrast, Paul says just the opposite: "We who are strong ought to put up with the failings of the weak, and not to please ourselves. Each of us must please our neighbor for the good purpose of building up the neighbor" (15:1-2).

Paul's teachings in Romans in general, and especially his ethical teachings in Romans 12:1–15:6, communicate a profound tenet of Pauline theology: *Right actions matter more than right beliefs.* And nothing illustrates this better than Paul's admonition to the strong that, though he personally believes their views about food and drink are theologically correct, they should not act in accord with that belief. Rather, they should eat in a manner not offensive to the weak. In other words, Paul instructs the community in Rome to follow the eating practices of the weak, in spite of the fact that the apostle himself is persuaded their view is wrong! According to Paul, being right about something—even a theological something—is not as important as living by an ethic of love.

In sum, Paul protested the inclination toward theological correctness that was starting to emerge among the community of believers. Given the often violent conflicts over doctrine that marked later Christian history, it is unfortunate that Paul's teachings on love and humility were not more influential.

# INVITATION TO DISCIPLESHIP

According to Paul's closing exhortations in Romans 12–15, the proper response to being made righteous by God is to live by an ethic of love (agape). The goal of this ethic of love is to build up others, which takes the shape of rejoicing with those who rejoice, weeping with those who weep, living in harmony with others, associating with the lowly, overcoming evil with good, and so on. For Paul to have accomplished his stated purpose among the Gentiles—namely bringing them to "the obedience of faith" (Romans 1:5)—that obedience must show itself in how they keep the law of love; for "love does no wrong to a neighbor; therefore, love is the fulfilling of the law" (Romans 13:10).

Paul clearly considered the new age of Christ to be coming soon (13:11-14), so his concluding words ring with urgency. He expects us to live toward the kingdom of God. He expects us to welcome one another in the spirit of Christ. He expects us not to pass judgment on each other. He expects us to pay taxes to whomever they are due. He expects us to feed even our enemies. He expects us to owe nothing but love to others. He expects that through faith, we will know God's righteousness and God's redemption and that we will live accordingly.

# FOR REFLECTION

- Where do you draw the line when it comes to faith and works? How does the church draw the line?

- Think of examples of individuals you know who express self-giving love in their lives. What main characteristics do they show?

- What picture comes to mind when you read Paul's use of the words *weak* and *strong* in Romans 14? What do you think is taking place in the Roman Christian community to prompt these words from Paul? How can either of these words characterize a person's faith?

# ENDNOTES

1. From *Against Apion,* II, 210, by Josephus, as found in *Josephus: The Life, Against Apion,* translated by H. St. J. Thackeray (Harvard University Press, 1926); pages 377–79.

2. From *Luther's Works: Career of the Reformer IV,* Vol. 34, edited by Lewis W. Spitz (Muhlenberg Press, 1960); page 337.

3. From *Augustine: Confessions and Enchiridion,* Vol. VII, translated and edited by Albert C. Outler (The Westminster Press, 1955); page 354.

4. From *Pelagius's Commentary on St. Paul's Epistle to the Romans,* translated by Theodore de Bruyn (Clarendon Press, 1993); page 94.

5. From *The Ante-Nicene Fathers: Translations of the Writings of the Fathers Down to A.D. 325,* Vol. IV, Origen de Principiis, edited by Alexander Roberts and James Donaldson (The Christian Literature Publishing Company, 1885); pages 260–61.

6. See *Romans in Full Circle: A History of Interpretation,* by Mark Reasoner (Westminster John Knox Press, 2005); pages 58–59.

7. From *Luther: Lectures on Romans,* in The Library of Christian Classics, Vol. XV, translated and edited by Wilhelm Pauck (The Westminster Press, 1951); page 208.

8. From *Letter to Simplicianus,* 2:21, by Augustine, as quoted in *Romans in Full Circle;* page 106.

9. From *A Greek-English Lexicon of the New Testament and Other Early Christian Literature,* fourth revised and augmented edition, by William F. Arndt and F. Wilbur Gingrich (The University of Chicago Press, 1957); pages 818–19.

10. From *Origen: An Exhortation to Martyrdom, Prayer, and Selected Works,* in The Classics of Western Spirituality, translated and edited by Rowan A. Greer (Paulist Press, 1979); page 73.